MARY ROSE

King Henry VIII's warship 1510–45

First published in December 2015

Brian Lavery has asserted his moral right to be
identified as the author of this work.

A catalogue record for this book is available
from the British Library.

ISBN 978 085733 511 1

Library of Congress control no. 2014957455

Published by Haynes Publishing,
Sparkford, Yeovil,
Somerset BA22 7JJ, UK.
Tel: 01963 440635
Int. tel: +44 1963 440635
Website: www.haynes.co.uk

Haynes North America Inc.,
861 Lawrence Drive,
Newbury Park,
California 91320, USA.

Printed in the USA by Odcombe Press LP,
1299 Bridgestone Parkway,
La Vergne, TN 37086.

Acknowledgements

This book would not have been possible without the co-operation
of the Mary Rose Trust, which is gratefully acknowledged. Special
thanks are due to the long-serving members Alexzandra Hildred and
Christopher Dobbs who gave much guidance and sourced many
illustrations; and who in addition checked the text and captions
meticulously and saved me from many mistakes, as well as providing
ideas. They, like other members of the Trust's staff, have many other
duties to perform and I am grateful to them for finding the time.
I learned much during my own spell as a member of the Trust's
publications committee a decade or so ago, though I regret that at
the time I was too involved in other work to develop many ideas.
However the extensive volumes produced under the supervision of
the committee have been the primary source for this book, along with
other works listed in the bibliography. But of course the main source
is the ship herself and the amazing collection of artefacts, with a large
selection now on display in the Mary Rose Museum.

Thanks are also due to John Lawson for the drawings, and to
Jonathan Falconer of Haynes for keeping faith during a long
gestation period.

MARY ROSE

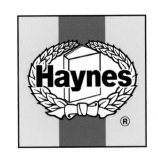

King Henry VIII's warship 1510–45

Owner's Workshop Manual

Insights into the construction, operation, excavation, recovery and restoration of a great Tudor ship and its contents

Brian Lavery

Contents

2 Acknowledgements

6 Introduction

7 The story of the Mary Rose

The First French War	11
The Second French War	15
The final battle	19

22 Anatomy of the Mary Rose

The hull	24
Carvel building	24
The shipwrights	25
The master frame and quarter frames	29
Bow and stern	31
Construction	36
Decks	44
The castles	53
Masts	54

58 The crew

Captains	61
Masters	61
The specialists	62
Seamen	64
The gunners	67
Soldiers	68
Duties	70
Life on board	71

78 Sailing the Mary Rose

Sailing qualities	82
The winds	82
Tides	84
The sails	86
Raising the anchor	89
Points of sailing	91
Steering	92
Decoration and flags	93
Navigation	94
Pilots	96
Coming to anchor	97

98 Fighting the Mary Rose

The ship of war	100
Going into battle	114

118 Recovering the Mary Rose

Early attempts	120
The Deane brothers	120
McKee and the rediscovery	122
The archaeology of the wreck	124
Towards the raising	127
Raising the Mary Rose	130

132 Conservation and display

Visitors	136
Conservation	137
Fund-raising	140
Continuing research and archaeology	141
The new museum	146

150 Appendix

Your route through the Mary Rose Museum	150

152 Bibliography

153 Index

OPPOSITE **Detail of the stern of the *Mary Rose*.**
(From an original painting by Geoff Hunt, PPRSMA)

Introduction

When the hull of the *Mary Rose* broke surface in the Solent in 1982 after 437 years underwater, it was watched by millions around the world. It was a seminal event in nautical archaeology, providing unique links with the Tudor past.

Crowds gathered on all the viewpoints round the Solent between Portsmouth and the Isle of Wight on Sunday 10 October 1982, anticipating the spectacle of a lifetime, even if the salvage vessel *Tog Mor* and its barge *TOW1* were just over a mile away from Southsea Castle and little could be seen with the naked eye. They expected a distant view of the Tudor flagship *Mary Rose* as she emerged from the sea after more than four centuries underwater. Television cameras and the world's press were much closer and ready to record the unique sight.

The British public had largely lost its passion for the sea and the navy over the previous three decades, but in the last few months the Falklands War had reminded the British and the rest of the world that sea power could still be important – indeed, the awards, including the first Victoria Crosses since 1969, were announced that Sunday, and the victory parade

was held in London two days later. The Tudor age had seen the birth of British sea power. The Falklands War seemed to mark a kind of conclusion to it – it did not seem likely that another independent British war against a sovereign nation with such a high naval content would ever happen again. And the early Tudor era, with its larger-than-life anti-hero, Henry VIII, always struck a chord with the public, after highly successful television series and films in the years before.

But that morning there was a delay; one of the legs of the lifting frame had bent more than 2ft out of position and the nylon strops used for the underwater transfer had not yet been replaced by the massive steel cables for the final lift. The operation was put back for another day. As a result, the crowds were much smaller on Monday 11th. But millions watched at home or on sets in TV rental shops as the ship finally broke the surface around nine in the morning. The slow raising was also seen by thousands of schoolchildren and their teachers. Reactions varied from awareness of a historic event, to 'I couldn't really tell what it was other than bits of rotten wood.' There was a heart-stopping moment just before midday. One mother was in the kitchen making food for her son's birthday when she heard a noise and raced back to the television 'as I thought *Mary Rose* was on her way to the bottom of the Solent'. It was far more serious for the archaeological director Margaret Rule. 'An unforgettable crunch was heard at the south-east corner of the ULF as a tubular pin used to restrain the leg had given way. … All hearts stopped but no damage had been done to the ship.' There was no

time for celebration. 'No one felt entirely safe, champagne went un-drunk and celebration cakes were uncut. Until we were safely in harbour no one was happy.' The rest of the population heard the result on programmes like the Six O'clock News, after they had got home from work and in all 60 million people are believed to have watched the event worldwide.

The Mary Rose was the standard topic of conversation in all sectors of society. Frank Johnson of The Times wrote an article on the fortunes of the Social Democratic Party under the headline 'The scuppered ship may surface yet', and he was not alone in making the comparison. Football supporters joked that a survivor was found on board, asking 'Have Arsenal scored yet?' The organisers had done their best to make the public aware that this was not an intact hull like the Vasa, which had been raised from Stockholm Harbour more than 20 years before, but the Mary Rose hull section, stripped of her decks and internal structures, looked very unimpressive lying in the steel cradle. Richard Ingrams wrote in The Spectator: 'Like the recapture of the Falkland Islands, the raising of the Mary Rose looked like a superbly efficient but ultimately pointless exercise.' It would take several decades to overcome this

scepticism, and show the Mary Rose to the public in a way that the old ship deserved.

Nineteenth-century historians often made extravagant claims about Henry VIII's foresight in naval warfare, and for the role of the Mary Rose as the forerunner of the battleship and the origin of British sea power. Many modern historians reject the idea that the king had planned the great expansion of the navy that began in his reign and continued until the 20th century – most of his reforms were reactive rather than far-sighted. And the Mary Rose was not the first true modern warship relying mainly on gun power. The gunport, which made heavy weapons viable, was already in use a decade or so before her launch, and the move to heavier gun armaments proceeded cautiously and haphazardly during her lifetime, as can be seen from the ship's own armament. But there is no denying the wreck's importance for archaeologists and historians, and its interest to millions of visitors over the years. If one was to choose a single ship to represent both a typical vessel of the epoch, and the development of the most advanced techniques, then it would be hard to better the Mary Rose. And beyond this, the wreck represents a single point in time, and gives a uniquely valuable picture of Tudor life, ashore as well as afloat.

ABOVE King Henry VIII wearing royal regalia with the Company of Barber Surgeons of London in 1540, painted by Hans Holbein. The barber-surgeons are wearing the type of cap that was recovered from the Mary Rose.

Chapter One

The story of the Mary Rose

The *Mary Rose* was a large and innovative warship when she was launched around 1510. She remained the largest purpose-built ship in the English fleet, apart from the *Henri Grace à Dieu* or *Great Harry*. She operated for more than thirty years, taking part in three different wars, though she never fought in a decisive battle.

OPPOSITE The *Mary Rose* was a successful warship in the service of King Henry VIII and fought in three wars.
(Detail from an original painting by Geoff Hunt, PPRSMA)

The story of the *Mary Rose* began more than 470 years earlier. The young King Henry VIII came to the throne on the death of his father, the first of the Tudor line to wear the crown. The new king soon rejected Henry VII's policy of maintaining peace and began to think of alliances for expansion. He did not look out across the Atlantic, as his father had done when sponsoring John Cabot's discovery of Newfoundland, but he had his eye on Europe where he still held Calais as a relic of the great empire built up by his hero, King Henry V, nearly a century earlier. France had been a traditional enemy, while an alliance with Spain was only natural as he was married to Catherine of Aragon, the daughter of Ferdinand and Isabella of Spain. Henry also had to look out for his brother-in-law James IV of Scotland, who was building a strong and modern navy for the only time in his country's history. In 1506 James's first 'great ship', the *Margaret*, was floated out at Leith. She was

of 600 or 700 tons and was named after James's wife and Henry's sister. The *Mary Rose* was likely a response to this. She was begun in 1510, was about 600 tons and was probably named after the Virgin Mary and her symbol of the rose; although it also had echoes of Henry's other sister, still unmarried, plus the Tudor emblem of a rose. It may or may not have been a subtle way to associate the Tudor line with divine providence.

By the end of July 1511 the *Mary Rose* and another new ship, the *Peter Pomegranate*, had been conveyed to the Thames for fitting out, presumably using some kind of jury or temporary rig, for in October Thomas Sperte the master and David Boner the purser were paid £66 13s 4d for 'all manner of stuff needful to be had for the decking and rigging of the same ship'. In December Sperte was paid again for 'all manner of charges concerning our said ship …'. She would be ready for sea that spring.

BELOW The activities of the fleet led by Sir Edward Howard in the *Mary Rose* during April to June 1512 included the capture of a few fishing boats and escorting the Marquis of Dorset's forces to invade Gascony.
(John Lawson)

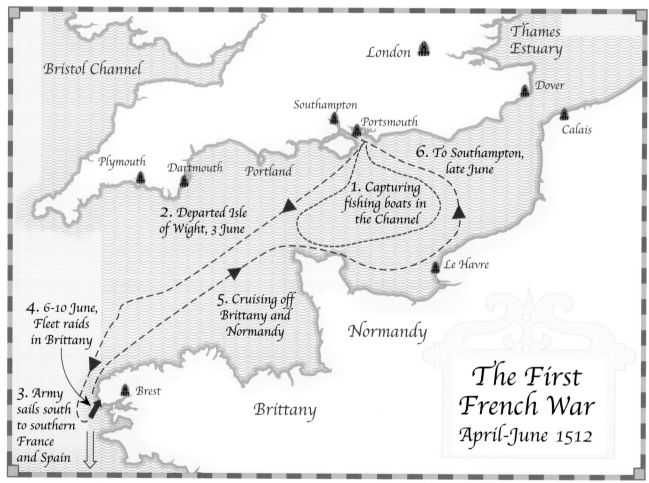

The First French War

In November 1511 Henry, seeking feudal glory, joined a Holy League against France. The winter was spent preparing the armed forces and ships, including the *Mary Rose*, for campaign. The English fleet was ready before the French, and in April and May 1512 it raided across the English Channel, with the *Mary Rose* as Sir Edward Howard's fleet flagship. The results were not decisive, but the fleet returned to the Solent to be reinforced by more ships, including the *Regent*, a larger vessel that had been built by Henry's father in 1487. At the end of May it sailed to escort an army of 12,000 men under the Marquis of Dorset to invade Gascony. It left them for the final part of their journey and began to operate in 'the trade', the area off Brest through which the ships of the Gascon wine trade had passed for centuries.

Brittany was only recently united with France through the marriage of King Louis XII with Anne of Brittany. Both had their own fleets, and very different views on naval tactics. The great natural harbour of Brest was largely undeveloped and lacked modern fortifications, so it offered fertile ground for English raids. On 6 June men landed in Bertheaume Bay just outside Brest Harbour and the men penetrated seven miles inland. The following day they raided the estate of the Breton commander Hervé de Porzmoguer, then headed a few miles south to attack the town of Le Conquet. On the 8th they landed on the Crozon peninsula to the south of Brest Harbour, where Breton troops retreated despite their superior numbers, perhaps because they were reluctant to engage an army that was supported by the Pope. Then the English fleet ranged along the northern French coast and, according to one account, they captured 26 Flemish and 40 Breton vessels. Next the *Mary Rose* led the fleet back to Portsmouth, with Howard claiming some success.

The fleet arrived back off Brest on 10 August,

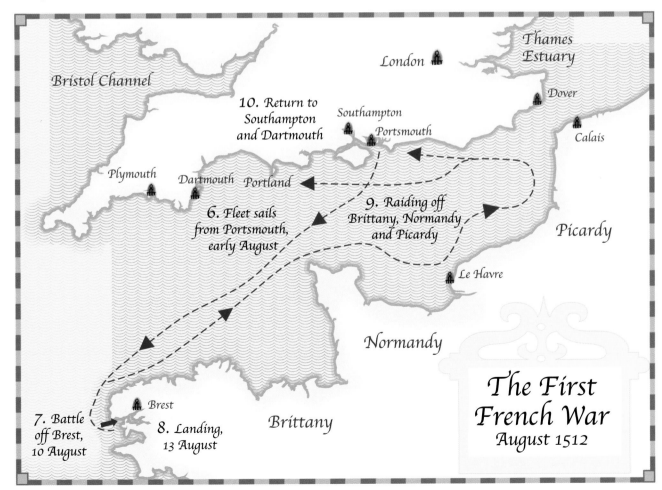

10. Return to Southampton and Dartmouth

6. Fleet sails from Portsmouth, early August

9. Raiding off Brittany, Normandy and Picardy

7. Battle off Brest, 10 August

8. Landing, 13 August

Bristol Channel

London

Thames Estuary

Dover

Calais

Southampton

Portsmouth

Plymouth

Dartmouth

Portland

Picardy

Le Havre

Normandy

Brest

Brittany

The First French War
August 1512

RIGHT The monastery that identified Pointe Saint-Mathieu according to the French edition of *Le Grand Routier* of 1502–10. Such landmarks were used by mariners for navigation, and a compass bearing on one could help to establish the ship's position.

St Lawrence's Day, but now the French were more prepared. Rounding Pointe Saint-Mathieu at the western end of the channel leading into the great harbour, at 11am the English lookouts sighted a fleet of 22 French and Breton ships anchored near the entrance, presumably in Bertheaume Bay. It was not common to seek battle in those days, but Howard showed 'extreme joy', and his *Mary Rose*, with the *Mary James* commanded by Anthony Ughtred, raced ahead to cut off the French retreat. The French flagship, the *Louise* under the direction

of René de Clermont, was seriously damaged by the fire from the *Mary Rose*'s bombards, with her mainmast broken and 300 men wounded, according to one account. The great Breton ship *Cordelière* was attacked by the *Mary James*. It is not clear whether the French had already begun their retreat before this attack, but they cut their anchor cables and sailed into Brest leaving two Breton ships, the *Cordelière* and the 'carrack of Brest', or *Queen*, to fight it out. The *Regent* under Sir Thomas Knyvet grappled and boarded the *Cordelière* and the English were apparently winning the hand-to-hand fighting when the magazine of the Breton ship exploded, whether by accident or design. All but six men of the Breton ship were killed, including the heroic Porzmoguer; 180 men survived from the *Regent*. Although Henry's all-powerful chief minister Cardinal Wolsey described the loss as 'lamentable and sorrowful tidings', the English were still left in control of the scene. They salvaged valuable anchors from the harbour, captured or burned 32 merchant ships and took 800 prisoners from landings. At the end of

RIGHT The raids in the peninsulas around the great natural harbour of Brest with English naval forces in red, land forces in white and French forces in blue. Some damage was done to French assets, but nothing decisive.
(John Lawson)

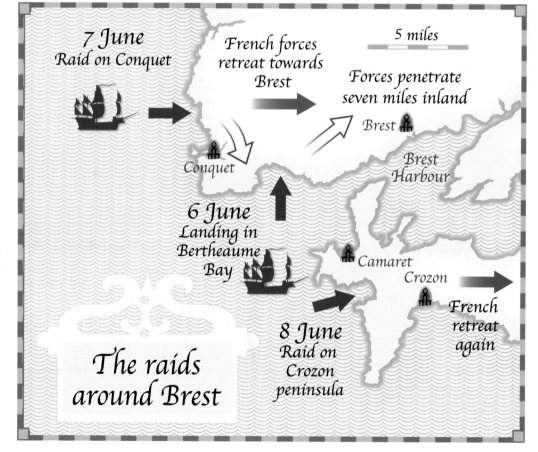

7 June
Raid on Conquet

French forces retreat towards Brest

5 miles

Forces penetrate seven miles inland

Brest

Conquet

Brest Harbour

6 June
Landing in Bertheaume Bay

Camaret

Crozon

8 June
Raid on Crozon peninsula

French retreat again

The raids around Brest

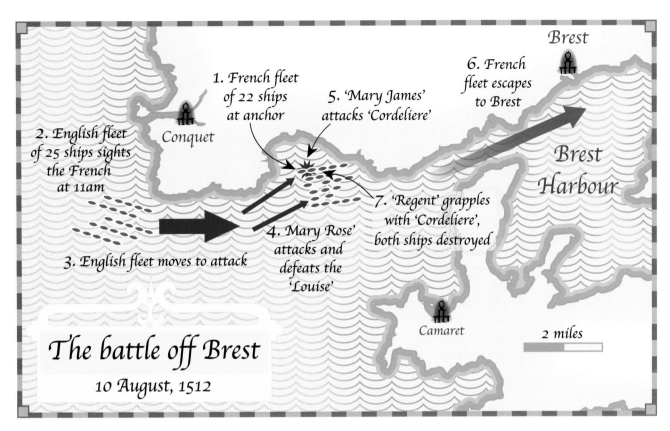

The battle off Brest
10 August, 1512

1. French fleet of 22 ships at anchor

2. English fleet of 25 ships sights the French at 11am

3. English fleet moves to attack

4. 'Mary Rose' attacks and defeats the 'Louise'

5. 'Mary James' attacks 'Cordeliere'

6. French fleet escapes to Brest

7. 'Regent' grapples with 'Cordeliere', both ships destroyed

Conquet

Brest

Brest Harbour

Camaret

2 miles

the month they returned to Southampton and Dartmouth. Again Henry was pleased; Howard was raised to the rank of Lord High Admiral (which was already planned), and rewarded with a grant of £66 13s 8d or a hundred marks 'for his good services upon the sea'.

It was the end of the summer campaign and at some stage in the autumn Thomas Sperte, master of the *Mary Rose*, and his colleague from the *Peter Pomegranate*, were summoned to meet the king at Eltham Palace in Kent 'for their mind in bestowing the King's ships this winter'. In October the *Mary Rose* was one of six ships ordered from Southampton to the River Thames. She lay at anchor in the river until the following March, when she demonstrated her sailing qualities to an ecstatic Howard in a voyage out of the estuary. The fleet was in Plymouth by 5 April 1513, ready for the next campaign. Howard was waiting for Spanish assistance, which never came, and he believed that a French fleet of 100 ships was almost ready to attack.

Indeed, the French fleet was far better prepared than the previous spring, and they had a different weapon. In the last decade or so the Venetians had found ways to mount

ABOVE The battle off Brest, 10 August 1512, the *Mary Rose*'s first taste of sea action against powerful naval forces. She led the attack and damaged the French *Louise*. *(John Lawson)*

LEFT Fire was the most terrifying danger to sailors in a wooden ship. The crew of the *Mary Rose* witnessed the English *Regent* and French *Cordelière* burning during the battle of 10 August, with heavy loss of life on both sides.

heavy guns known as basilisks in the bows of their galleys. They were far more powerful than the numerous but light guns used in northern Europe, and their oars gave them a mobility that was denied to the sailing ship, at least in light winds and smooth seas. Galleys, of course, had their disadvantages – they were low, lightly built and could not cope with strong winds, so the French force under Pregent de Bidoux had failed to raid England as planned, and had spent much of its time sheltering from bad weather on the north coast of Brittany. Its crews, not necessarily slaves or convicts, were exposed to the elements during the voyage and many of them fell ill. Pregent had to get convicts from the prisons of Angers, and recruited 200 men locally. Meanwhile, the English had tried to fit out their own galley force but had limited experience and no great supply of oarsmen, although Captain William Sabine would argue that there were many convicts who would rather die in action than suffer a shameful death on the gallows.

The English fleet sailed from Plymouth on 10 April 1513. They arrived off Brest where a French fleet of 15 sailing ships fled into the harbour 'like cowards' according to Howard. An attempt to attack the French in Brest failed when the *Nicholas of Hampton*,

commanded by Arthur Plantagenet, struck a rock and 'burst asunder'. The fleet scoured the coast again and raided Crozon Bay. Then on 22 April the French galleys arrived from their ineffectual voyage in the north of Brittany to change the picture. According to Edward Echyngham: '6 galleys and 4 foists came through part of the King's navy, and they sank the ship that was Master Compton's, and strake through one of the King's new barks, the which Sir Stephen Bull is captain of, in seven places, they that was within the ship had much pain to hold her above the water.' The galleys then anchored in Blanc-Sablon or White Sands Bay with their heavy guns facing outward and their flanks protected by guns on shore. Howard rejected the idea of hauling guns over the narrow peninsula to attack the galleys from behind and launched a daring, even reckless, assault in which he was killed. His fleet retreated in some disorder. There is no sign that the *Mary Rose* had been damaged or even directly engaged in these fights, but the fear of galleys was to have a huge influence on her future career.

Howard's elder brother Thomas was appointed Lord High Admiral and arrived in Plymouth 'as weary of riding as any man ever was'. On board the *Mary Rose* he assembled 'my lord Ferrers and all other noblemen and captains and most expert masters of your army' and asked why they had retreated. Most of them replied that they were desperately short of victuals, a common problem with Henry's fleets, so they could not sustain a long campaign. But on the same day Thomas reported to Cardinal Wolsey: 'Never saw men in greater fear than all the masters and mariners be of the galleys, insomuch that in a manner they had lief to go into purgatory as to the Trade.' They were 'the worst ordered army and farthest out of rule' that he had ever seen. The fleet was trapped in Plymouth for nine days and Thomas longed to get to Southampton where more supplies were available. In the meantime some of his soldiers were 'abroad in the country and rob [and] steal and do much hurt'. He intended to set up gallows on shore 'to hang half a dozen knaves' as a deterrent to the rest.

After reaching Southampton by 5 June,

BELOW The kind of battle that Henry's sailors feared, with a sailing warship attacked by several galleys at Messina, as drawn by Huys after Bruegel in 1561. The galleys, though very vulnerable to gunfire, could attack from any angle in light winds, and deploy their forward-firing guns.
(Rijksmuseum, Amsterdam)

Thomas had his ships re-victualled but there were still problems with discipline. Many men had tried to desert and Hereford Gaol was full of those who failed. He planned to hang two of them if the case against them should be proved. But at the same time he had ideas for a new attack on France, which might have succeeded. The French sailing ships were timidly led and it was believed they would do nothing without the support of their Scottish and Danish allies, while the galleys were short of men again as their crews succumbed to illness. However, the war took another turn. Henry decided to concentrate his attack on northern France by way of Calais and had a certain amount of success in a cavalry action known as the Battle of the Spurs, which allowed him to take the town of Thérouanne. James IV of Scotland finally declared war in support of his French allies and the *Mary Rose* was one of the ships sent up the North Sea to counter a move by James's formidable fleet. She spent four days in Hull and sixteen in Newcastle but the Scottish fleet took the more hazardous route round the north and west to join the French. Moreover, the Scottish army suffered a shattering defeat on Flodden Field on 9 September 1513 and James was killed, leaving his infant son as king.

The *Mary Rose* was laid up again during the winter and was recommissioned under Sir Henry Sherburn. There was a plan to attack Pregent's galleys near Cherbourg, but the war ended with an Anglo-French truce in July. Anne of Brittany had died in January, so to secure the peace Henry's favourite sister Mary, after whom the *Mary Rose* had perhaps been named, was married to Louis XII and became Queen of France. Louis died after less than three months, worn out it was said, by a bride a third of his age.

The Second French War

Perhaps the most radical of Henry's naval policies was the decision to keep his ships in good condition now the war was over – previous great navies, such as those assembled by King John and Henry V had been left to rot when they were no longer needed. The *Mary Rose* was laid up at Blackwall on the Thames in July 1514. An inventory was taken of her stores,

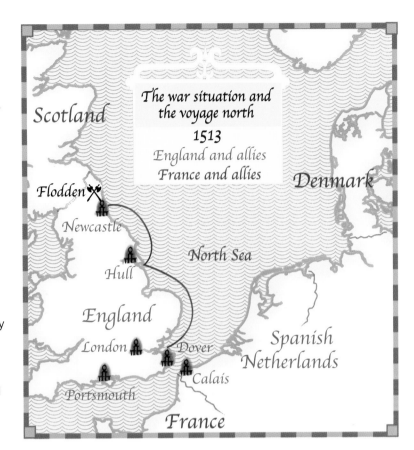

ABOVE The war situation and the *Mary Rose*'s voyage north in 1513. The campaign against Scotland was effectively ended when her army under James IV was defeated at Flodden and *Mary Rose* saw no action.
(John Lawson)

and she was put in the care of shipkeepers. To avoid the constant grounding caused by the rise and fall of tides in the river, Henry was building a wet dock at Deptford, a few miles upriver. John Hopton, the Clerk Comptroller of the King's Ships, was contracted to build 'a good and able pond' near the king's storehouse at Deptford Strond, 'wherein shall ride at all times afloat … the *Great Galley*, the *Mary Rose*, the *Peter Pomegranate*, the *Great Bark* and the *Lesser Bark*'. In June 1520 Henry sailed to Calais to meet Francis I of France at the famous Field of the Cloth of Gold. The *Mary Rose* was one of the ships put into commission to 'scour the seas from time to time during the passage of the King', who travelled in a smaller ship that could enter Dover and Calais harbours.

The negotiations with Francis failed to find any lasting peace, and in 1522 Henry joined an alliance with Charles V, now extremely powerful

as Holy Roman Emperor as well as King of Spain. In May Charles visited England and went on board the *Mary Rose* at Dover. War was declared and again the English navy was ready for action first. Sir Thomas Howard, now the Earl of Surrey, used the *Mary Rose* as his flagship once more. He planned to attack Le Havre, but was constrained by lack of supplies – Surrey was 'doubting much more of victuals than wind'.

Instead they chose a softer target. On 1 July 1522 the fleet entered the narrow, rocky waters of Morlaix Bay to raid the town of that name, rich from trade. Soldiers were landed on the east bank of the river, along with 14 light guns known as falcons. These weighed from 550 to 750lb and fired a ball of 1¾ to 2⅛lb. The *Mary Rose* herself had carried two falcons in 1514. The soldiers dragged the guns five miles along the riverbank, driving off local forces on the way. They reached the outskirts of the town and Surrey led an assault. The soldiers 'fell to

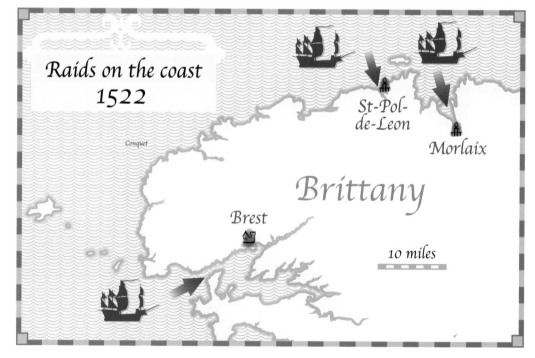

RIGHT Raids on the coast in 1522 during the Second French War. Some French shipping was destroyed and houses were burned in Brest, but little damage was done to naval forces. *(John Lawson)*

Raids on the coast 1522

Conquet

St-Pol-de-Leon

Morlaix

Brittany

Brest

10 miles

pillage and rifled the chests and warehouses of merchants' until they had 'more than they could bear away'. French sources suggest that many of them got drunk, which allowed some kind of counter-attack, but at six o'clock they began to withdraw, setting light to the town and any villages on the way back. Next day 'all men were shipped and few or none missed'. Some 16 or 17 small ships in the river were burned and on the 3rd Surrey wrote to Wolsey: 'Scribbled in the *Mary Rose*, within the haven of Morlaix.' The fleet moved a short distance along the coast to Saint-Pol-de-Léon where the smaller ships and ships' boats attempted an attack but were driven off by Breton guns. They destroyed a ship of 200 tons and several smaller ones, then sailed 50 miles round the coast to enter the great harbour of Brest, where barks and row-barges landed men who burned houses in the town, but did not attempt to take the strong castle at the mouth of the River Penfeld. They were ordered back and anchored off Cowes on the Isle of Wight. On 21 July Surrey reported to the king, 'of whom he was well welcomed you may be sure'.

The war with France concluded in 1525 and in the following year the *Mary Rose* was in the care of eight shipkeepers. Like several other ships she was 'good for the wars, or else for the King's pleasure, but their overlops [decks], summer castles, and decks must be caulked shortly after March'. In accordance with Henry's policy of maintaining his ships she was repaired in 1527 by the 'caulking of her overlop & decks fore and aft within board and likewise for searching and caulking from the keel upward without board and repairing and trimming of her boat …'. Henry was expanding Portsmouth Dockyard, including

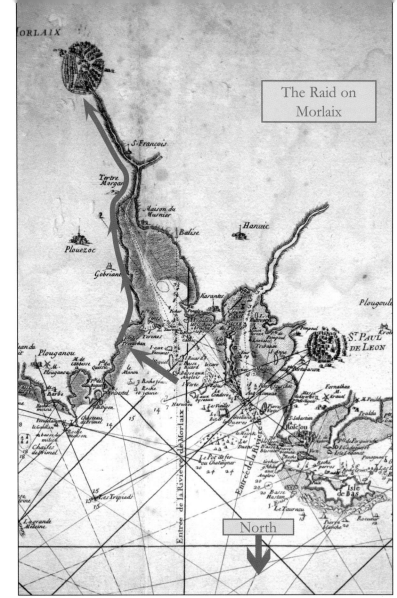

ABOVE The raid on Morlaix showing the main towns, some of the numerous navigational hazards, the approximate position of the anchorage of the English fleet and the route taken by the raiders. *(National Maritime Museum)*

BELOW A drawing of a damaged bronze falcon from around 1520, in the Royal Armouries. Light guns such as these could be landed and dragged by soldiers, as in the raid on Morlaix.

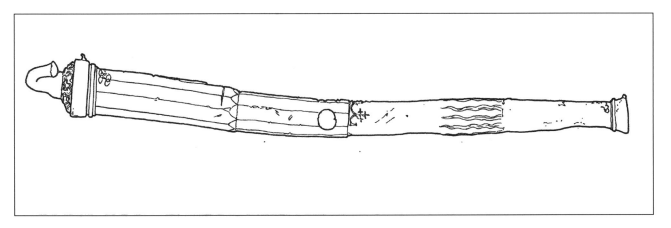

RIGHT The only surviving picture of the *Mary Rose*, from Anthony Anthony's roll of 1546, after she had sunk. Anthony was an ordnance officer and was more concerned with guns. Questionably, he places the main yard aft of the mast. His interpretation of the layout of the hull and guns is perhaps more trustworthy and it also shows the great array of flags and pennants that a Tudor warship might carry. *(Pepys Library, Magdalene College, Cambridge)*

a new dock 'for the grounding of the *Mary Rose*, the *Peter Pomegranate*, and the *John Baptist'*. After that the ship disappears from the records for several years.

Invasion of England became a real possibility from 1534 when Henry completed his break from the Roman Church to the fury of both France and Spain, although it was some years before they could muster a suitable force to oppose him. Henry's finances had a great boost from the treasures of the dissolved monasteries, but he chose to spend it on coastal fortifications along the south coast, including Southsea Castle near Portsmouth. In 1536 he began to acquire a few more ships for the navy, and armaments for them. The *Mary Rose* was rebuilt and the evidence of her timbers shows that she had some new internal framing and knees. By January 1539, according to the powerful minister Thomas Cromwell she was one of three ships in the Thames that was 'new made, standing in their docks there, masts ready but not set up, who cannot be made ready to sail in under three months' time after commandment given'. The *Mary Rose* was still in the Thames in mid-1539 when members of her crew had some trouble. Robert Grygges of Ipswich, William Oram of London and a man named Marmaduke (the only ordinary crewmen of the *Mary Rose* whose names appear in written records) 'sat making merry' in a house at Deptford. They failed to attract the attention of the men still on

board to have a boat sent out for them, so they commandeered a wherry but were driven against a Portuguese ship at anchor. A fight started, the English sailors boarded, and Oram was injured in the head. The original deposition survives but the outcome of a court case in June 1539 is not known.

The dockyard officials tried to resist Henry's attempt to fit yet more guns to the *Mary Rose's* ageing hull. She already had 'over the luff two whole slings lying quarter-wise'; that is, firing forward from the triangular castle in the bows. Furthermore at the 'barbican head' or the break of the quarterdeck there were two culverins firing forward past the forecastle, with two sakers on the deck above. No more forward-firing armament could be fitted without 'the taking away of two knees and the spoiling of the clamps that beareth the bitts, which will be a great weakening to the same part of the ship'.

There was no real repeat of the *Mary Rose* concept in Henry's fleet. New building since 1515 had mainly been of galleys, mostly very small. Other large ships in the fleet of 1545 had been bought or hired from various foreign sources. Tonnage measurement was always variable in those days, and in 1545 the *Mary Rose* was now rated at 800 tons, which may or may not reflect an increase in her weight, bringing her gunports closer to the waterline. She was second behind the *Henri Grace à Dieu* or *Great Harry* at 1,000 tons and rivalled only by

the *Gabriel Royal*, a Genoese carrack, the *Great Bark* or *Great Galley*, which had been rebuilt in 1538 and the *Jesus of Lubeck* hired from the Hansa League of northern Germany.

The final battle

Henry was at war with Scotland and in February 1543 he signed an alliance with Charles V against France and a new war began in June. The English conquered Boulogne in the following year, but Charles V made his peace with France leaving Henry to fight on alone. The *Mary Rose* was evidently not sent to sea for the early campaigns, but in July 1545 she joined Viscount Lisle, the Lord High Admiral, with a fleet of 80 ships. They sailed for Portsmouth but were trapped inside the harbour due to the

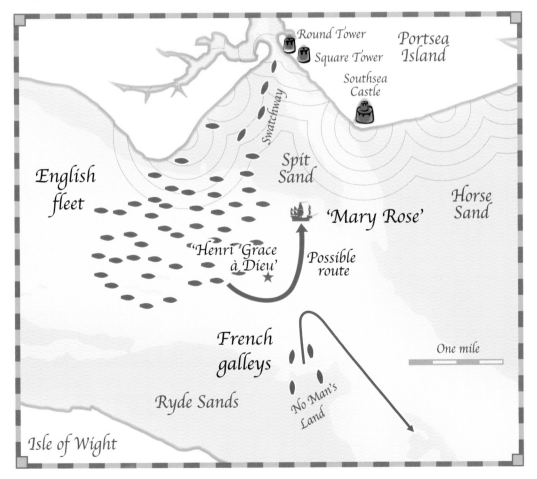

LEFT A modern reconstruction of the route of the *Mary Rose* just before her sinking. The main English fleet is formed up at Spithead and some ships are still coming out of the harbour. The sharp turns by the *Mary Rose* may have contributed to her sinking. Based on a drawing by Dr Dominic Fontana of the University of Portsmouth.
(John Lawson)

ABOVE The Cowdray engraving shows the situation just after the *Mary Rose* sank. The original was destroyed in a fire at Cowdray House in 1793, so we are reliant on a copy published by the Society of Antiquaries in 1778. As well as the sinking it shows much detail of the battle, and the arrival of the king at Southsea Castle in the centre.

lack of wind. Meanwhile, the French mobilised a force of 150 to 200 ships, including 25 galleys, which were no longer needed in the Mediterranean after the peace with Charles V. They raided Brighton on 18 July, then entered the Solent the next day, landing troops on the Isle of Wight. Henry was dining on board one of the ships when the alarm was raised, and preparations were made. That morning there was no wind, which was ideal for the galleys. A breeze sprang up in the afternoon and the fleet, perhaps led by the *Mary Rose,* was able to get under way. With their recent improvements the English ships were better equipped to deal with galleys, and the French were forced to retreat. The *Mary Rose* and the *Henri Grace à Dieu* were in the forefront of the attack; the former apparently headed south-east to fire on the enemy, then turned to the north to find space to reload. She came under fire herself, although the later French claim that she was seriously damaged is not substantiated. As she approached the Spitsand Bank off Portsmouth she made a turn and capsized, with fatal results.

The question of why the *Mary Rose* sank is a perennial one, and will probably never be fully resolved. There are at least half a dozen factors to be taken into account, each of which may have contributed to the loss. The extra guns of

LEFT Geoff Hunt's reconstruction of the ship capsizing, with most of the crew trapped under anti-boarding nettings in the waist – in any case, not many of them could swim and there were few boats to rescue them. (*Geoff Hunt, PPRSMA*)

earlier and more recent refits had added to her weight and brought the gunports dangerously close to the waterline. Some were fitted well up in the ship, which would have reduced her stability. According to some reports she was also carrying extra crew, mostly soldiers who would have been stationed high up with weapons and armour and that would also have reduced stability. Charles V's ambassador François van der Delft spoke to a survivor who told him that the guns had just been fired on one side and the ship was turning to fire the other side. This was normal procedure at the time and is partly borne out by the archaeological evidence. The port-side guns (as recovered by the Deanes) were apparently all loaded and the starboard ones were probably in the process of reloading. The turn was probably carried out because the ship was coming dangerously close to the shallow waters of Spitsand.

There is evidence of lack of discipline and coordination on board. Sir George Carew's remark that he had 'a sort of knaves, whom he could not rule' might indicate a lack of discipline. It has also been suggested that the large number of foreigners identified on board by archaeological evidence might have led to misunderstanding – although it seems likely that most of them were mercenary soldiers rather than sailors. In any case, the gunports on both sides were open when the turn took place, and

the ship was evidently struck by a sudden gust of wind. She began to heel over to starboard and water rushed in through the open ports causing a capsizing motion. Most of the men were trapped under the boarding nettings and around 500 were lost. Some 30 or 40 men, probably those in the rigging, were saved and the only surviving picture of the loss shows one of them clinging desperately to the mast. Henry himself witnessed the tragedy from the shore and the French were cheered by it. But their invasion plan faltered and they withdrew without any other material gain.

BELOW A detail from the Cowdray engraving, showing the fore and main mast of the *Mary Rose* still above the water, crew members floating, dead or drowning despite the boats coming to the rescue. Southsea Castle is in the foreground.

Chapter Two

Anatomy of the Mary Rose

The wooden hull of the *Mary Rose,* though largely eroded during her time underwater, provides many insights into the building methods of the time. It has also inspired study of design techniques, while some of the artefacts tell us about her masts and rigging.

OPPOSITE In earlier periods north European ships mostly had clinker-built hulls with overlapping planks and the frame timbers fitted afterwards. However, the *Mary Rose* had a carvel-built hull with planks laid edge-to-edge to give a smooth finish. They were laid on a structure of stout frames, which was built first and can be seen here. *(Courtesy Stephen Foote)*

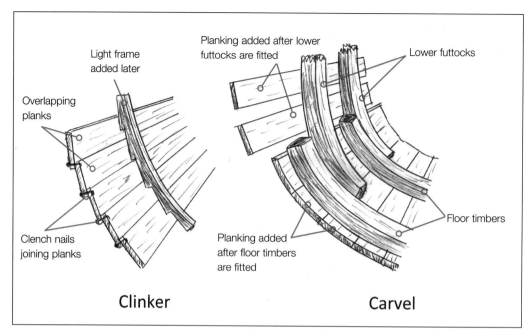

Clinker / Carvel

The hull

The precise date when the *Mary Rose* was begun is unknown, but it seems likely that she and the *Peter Pomegranate* (named after the badge of Henry's wife Catherine of Aragon) were those referred to in a document signed by Henry VIII on 29 January 1510, ordering two new ships. (This was a tradition already established by Henry VII, who had begun the *Regent* and *Sovereign* soon after his own accession in 1485.) Neither is it known for certain where the new ships were built. A letter from the Venetian ambassador refers to four ships being constructed at Hampton,

or Southampton, in December 1509, but no further details are given. The new dockyard at Portsmouth is a slightly more likely site, for in July 1511 payments were made for conveying the newly completed *Mary Rose* from there to the Thames. A ship of this size and weight was perhaps raised in a dry dock, which would avoid some of the problems associated with a building slipway – it could be assembled with the frames upright rather than angled slightly downwards, as with a slip, and this would make it easier to ensure they were vertical. If it was floated out from a dock it would not be necessary to support it on a special cradle during launching, or to build launch-ways out into the water, as with a slipway. The dock was probably a simple purpose-built hole near the shoreline, and its seaward end was only breached when the ship was ready to float. As late as 1562, 'labourers, marshmen and others' were paid for the construction of three new ships at Deptford, including 'opening of the dockhead for the launching of the same'.

Carvel building

It was only in the last 50 years that English shipwrights had begun to learn carvel building, with planks laid side by side, instead of their more traditional system of clinker, with overlapping planks nailed together. This was a huge change for a conservative profession,

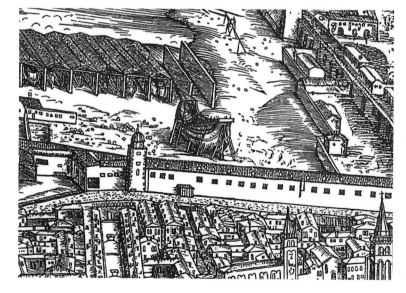

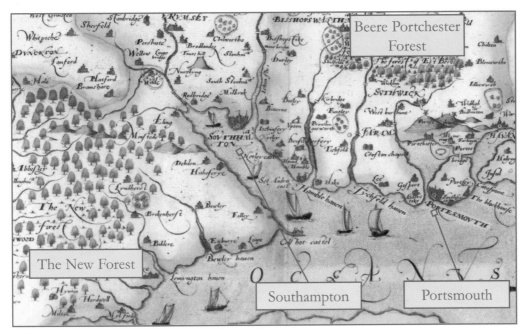

Beere Portchester
Forest

The New Forest

Southampton

Portsmouth

LEFT Hampshire, from Christopher Saxton's map of 1575, showing the New Forest and Beere Portchester forest, which may well have supplied timber for the *Mary Rose*. The ports of Southampton and Portsmouth are also shown, along with the Isle of Wight, which provided shelter for the anchorage of Spithead off Portsmouth.

and it had many implications. Shipwrights had to place much greater emphasis on the frame rather than the planking of the ship, but paradoxically the new system allowed them to use much thicker planks, and therefore build bigger ships. They had to leave a small gap between successive rows or 'strakes' of planks so that they could be caulked by forcing oakum, or loose pieces of rope, between them and sealing the joint with pitch or tar. Most important of all, carvel building needed much more pre-planning as the heavy frame pieces were cut out – not necessarily using plans in the modern sense of the term, but with some method of drawing out the shape before cutting.

Carvel building had long been the standard method in the Mediterranean and Portugal, and it is quite likely that foreign shipwrights, perhaps Spaniards or Venetians, had some influence on the design of the new ship. Plans were almost certainly not used, but the master shipwright probably had a clear idea of what was to be done, based on his experience. There is no evidence that models were employed as part of the process, although by the 1570s it was suggested they might be an aid to measure tonnage. The design and construction of the ship proceeded in unison, but the proportions would have to be established early. Most shipwrights had a formula based on the length of the keel to maximum breadth. In the case of the *Mary Rose* the keel was approximately

106ft or 32.31m long, while the breadth was around 39ft 4in, or 11.98m. This gives a ratio of 1:2.7, well within the normal range of 1:2 for bulky merchant ships and 1:3 for fast warships.

The shipwrights

The skilled workers who put a ship together were the shipwrights. All shipwrights, like the seamen of the day, nominally started equal, with skills in both designing and building ships, but already there are signs that those with the right parentage were more likely to take part in design and management. In 1544 the king's shipwright

BELOW Examples of how ship's timbers might be selected from particular trees, including varieties of straight timber for keels, planks, masts and pillars and more valuable curved or compass timber for futtocks and knees. *(John Lawson)*

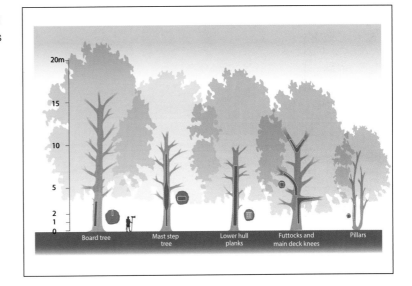

James Baker took on his son Matthew, who later produced our most detailed drawings of Elizabethan ships. Unlike seamen, shipwrights had to serve an apprenticeship and this was strictly enforced by bodies such as local guilds. Again like seamen (and indeed like all the king's subjects), shipwrights could be pressed into royal service. They were assisted in their work by sawyers, by the relatively new trade of caulker to fill the spaces between the planks, and by labourers to clear the dock and move timbers into place. There was no great concentration of shipwrights, as developed later in the royal dockyards, so they had to be gathered from afar for a major ship. For the larger *Great Harry* they came from Devon, Bristol, East Anglia and Yorkshire. Some 164 of the men who built the *Mary Rose* and *Peter Pomegranate* were given coats worth 2s to 5s each, and they were put up in accommodation with flock beds. Cooks were employed to prepare fish, peas and oatmeal for them.

The records provide very little information on the practices and customs of shipwrights of the period, but we know something about their tools from the contents of the *Mary Rose*'s carpenters' chests, for the two professions were essentially one. There is no sign of the large two-man frame saw that could be used to cut tree trunks into futtocks or planks, although one can be seen on a French manuscript of the late 15th century, with the wood propped up on trestles and an upper and lower sawyer. Nor is there an example of the heavier two-man saw seen in the *Book of Trades* of 1568, this time cutting the timber across the grain. Such tools were needed for heavy work in shipyards but were less necessary for the running repairs to be carried out on board. The handles of much smaller saws have been found, though the steel blades have rusted away.

The *Mary Rose* carpenters used lines on reels to mark out straight lines, presumably covering them with chalk, stretching them across the surface to be cut and pinging them to produce a mark – a process which remained familiar in the 20th century. They could draw circles with the same implements, with a nail at each end of a string. The classic shipwright's tool was the adze, a kind of axe with the blade set at right angles to the handle, instead of in line with it. Those from the *Mary Rose* were of the 'stirrup adze' type, with a heavy wooden part of the handle locking the blade in place. The adze was used to trim wood, for example in 'bevelling' the frame timbers or trimming them finally to shape, or providing a smoother finish to the hull planking. Conventional axes were also used for cutting.

Drilling was an important aspect of the shipwright's work, particularly to make holes in the planks and frames for trenails and bolts. A brace was used to make smaller holes or perhaps to sink pilot holes for the larger ones, but the holes for the trenails and other fastenings were made by an auger, a straight piece of wood with a handle on each end and a recess in the centre. The shipwright fitted a bit to it, not a twist drill as in modern times,

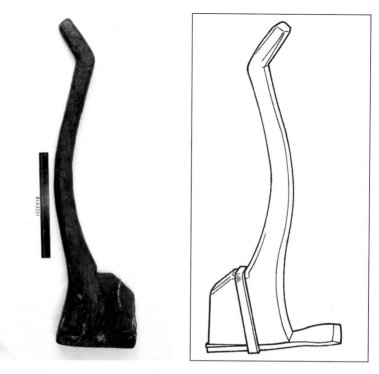

ABOVE The wooden part of a 'stirrup' adze as recovered from the ship, with the iron part reconstructed in the line drawing. This was the characteristic shipwright's tool and was used to hew and 'dub' timbers for their final trimming to shape, before or after fitting to the hull.

BELOW LEFT A brace, an alternative to the auger for drilling smaller holes, similar in principle to tools still used today.

BELOW The handle of an auger. The iron bit would be fitted in the recess shown in the centre in the lowest drawing. Using one was hard work, partly because the operator had to apply pressure as well as turning it.

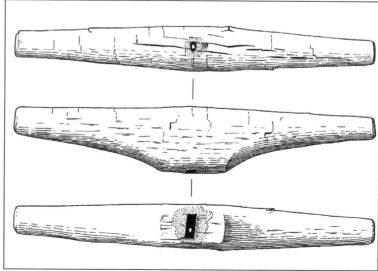

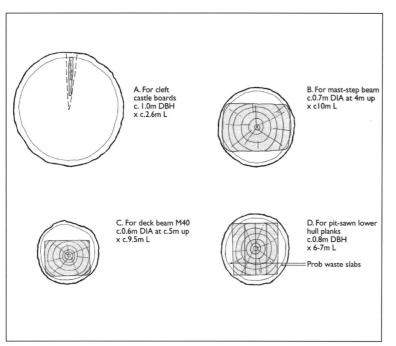

A. For cleft castle boards c. 1.0m DBH x c.2.6m L

B. For mast-step beam c.0.7m DIA at 4m up x c10m L

C. For deck beam M40 c.0.6m DIA at c.5m up x c.9.5m L

D. For pit-sawn lower hull planks c.0.8m DBH x 6-7m L
— Prob waste slabs

ABOVE Ways of cutting a tree for different purposes, from a drawing by Damien Goodburn. Radial cutting, as shown in the upper left, provided planks with stronger grain for clinker building. It was falling into disuse by Tudor times but the cleft boards in the upper castle of the *Mary Rose* were cut from the tree using this method.

BELOW The principles of radial cutting, as normally used for clinker building to make the best use of the grain of the timber. The wood was split by wedges and then trimmed by axe.

but a hollow semicircular shell. He pressed it down with his arms and twisted by hand. This was especially heavy work. Two centuries later, when Mary Lacey disguised herself as a man to work in the royal dockyards, she came closest to discovery when she did not have the strength to operate an auger. Some of the other items found in the *Mary Rose*, such as planes and spokeshaves, were more appropriate for joinery work among the cabins and furniture, rather than the heavier tasks of cutting the frames and fitting the planks of a great ship.

Curved-frame timbers were probably cut flat, or 'sided' in one plane then left for the shipwrights to select them for the appropriate curve. After that they were cut to the curved shape, perhaps being bevelled in places near the bow and stern where the hull tended to

BELOW The keel would normally be straight but it has become distorted or hogged over the years. It is shown here in side view with its three components and the overlaps, or scarfs, between them. It was not square in cross section, but was narrower towards the bottom. The apron to the right is the first part of the knee that supports the head and begins the upward curve.

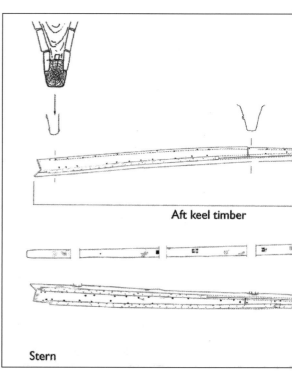

Aft keel timber

Stern

narrow. Planks were usually cut in horizontal or vertical slices, but the older method, of radial cutting, was used for clinker building, which survived in the upper part of the hull.

The master frame and quarter frames

The construction of the ship began with the keel, a straight piece of timber made in three pieces joined by scarfs, 300mm deep and 380mm wide in midships, tapering to 150mm at its forward end. In the wreck, perhaps as the result of repairs, the middle section is of oak and the others of elm, which produced straighter timber. During construction it was laid on a row of blocks inside the dock, or on the building slip if that was used. The sternpost, fitted at the after end of the keel, had a straight rear face to hold the rudder and was angled backwards at 72°. It had to bear a good deal of stress so it was backed up by a 'false sternpost'

RIGHT The use of segments of circles, or 'sweeps' to form the master frame of the *Mary Rose.* The numbers are the diameters of the sweeps in feet.

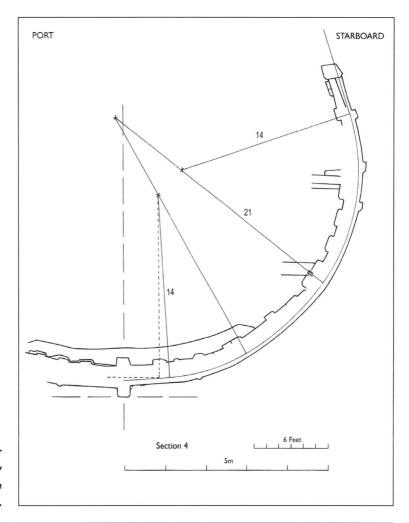

PORT   STARBOARD

14

21

14

Section 4

6 Feet

5m

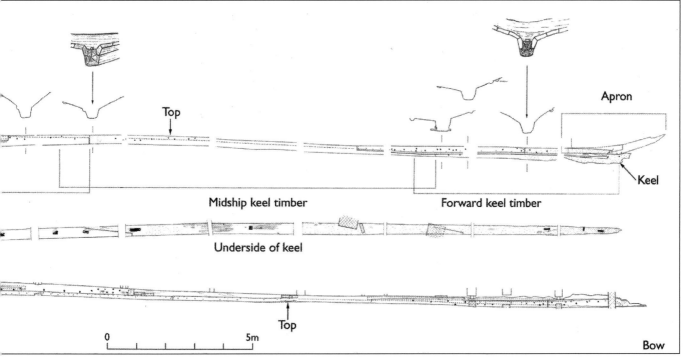

Top

Midship keel timber

Forward keel timber

Apron

Keel

Underside of keel

Top

0   5m

Bow

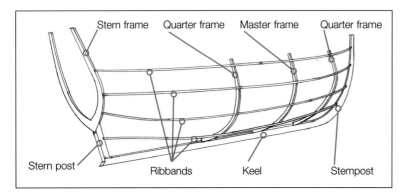

Stern frame   Quarter frame   Master frame   Quarter frame

Stern post   Ribbands   Keel   Stempost

ABOVE The master frame, quarter frames and ribbands (shown on the starboard side only). This is purely schematic, it does not necessarily show the actual shape of the bow and stern. There is no attempt to reveal the different futtocks that make up each frame, and there is no stage when the ship would look exactly like this, as the lower level was probably planked before the upper futtocks were in place.

and a stern knee inside the hull. The forward end of the keel was surmounted by the stempost, a curved shape with a radius of around 30ft or 9m made from at least two principal timbers joined together by scarfs, with the 'apron' mimicking its shape internally and adding extra strength.

The most important component in forming the shape of the hull was the 'master frame' in the centre of the ship. This was drawn by means of a series of arcs of circles, forming tangents with one another. In the case of the *Mary Rose,* there was a short flat section 4ft wide on each side of the keel, known as the floor. Then came the first curve, the bilge arc or floor sweep, 14ft in radius. This created a distinctive bulge in the hull form, and perhaps it is no coincidence that the word 'bilge' began to enter the English language around the beginning of the 16th century with the development of this kind of hull shape. There

was another 14ft-radius segment of a circle on either side of the maximum breadth just above, and these were joined by a further curve of 21ft known as the futtock arc. These dimensions were reflected in most of the frames throughout the ship – the same radii were generally used, although the length of each segment might vary. Above the maximum breadth the hull tapered inwards, a system known as 'tumble-home'. This was probably intended to reduce topweight by using shorter deck beams and other timbers, and to make it easier for the crew to move from side to side when working on the upper decks.

The shape of the rest of the hull was largely controlled by two more frames forward and aft of the master frame. These were the quarter frames, on which most of the others were modelled. They were approximately 22ft or 6.7m forward and aft of the master frame. During construction these were joined by battens or 'ribbands' (rib-bands), which held them in place but also guided the shape of the frames between. The ribbands extended forward to join the curved stempost, and aft to be attached to the sternpost and the stern frame.

More mathematical shipwrights might have also used more sophisticated systems to aid in forming the shape. A system of 'rising' and 'narrowing' lines was emerging. The narrowing line, of the floor or the maximum breadth, started in midships and curved inwards towards the bow

RIGHT This system, used on the Matthew Baker drafts of *c*1575, is probably more sophisticated than what was available when the *Mary Rose* was built. The master and quarter frames are still given prominence, but 'rising' and narrowing lines are used to determine the shape of the hull between them. In fact, the rising and narrowing lines were the same line, but seen in different planes.

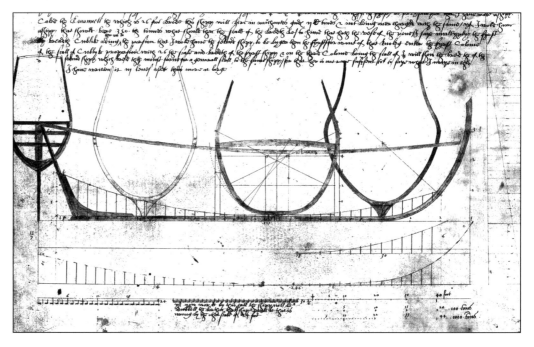

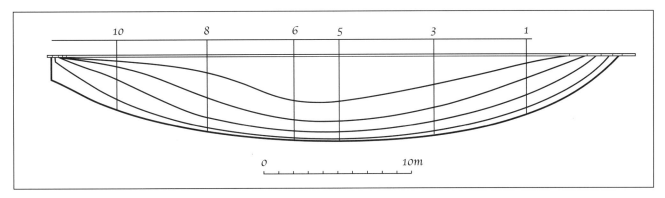

10   8   6 5   3   1

0   10m

ABOVE The reconstructed waterlines of the *Mary Rose*, displaying the 'fairness' of the hull – although such a technique would not have been used at the time. The drawing shows a distinctive bulge just aft of midships. Aft of that, the lower hull narrows towards the rudder. *(John Lawson)*

BELOW A projected bow shape of the *Mary Rose,* though it might be too fine *(below).* Here it is compared with that of Nelson's *Victory* of 1765 *(bottom).* After two centuries of development and greatly increased gun power, the latter ship had much fuller lines, able to support the weight of heavy guns. The increase in armament on a relatively fine hull may well have contributed to the *Mary Rose*'s sinking. *(John Lawson)*

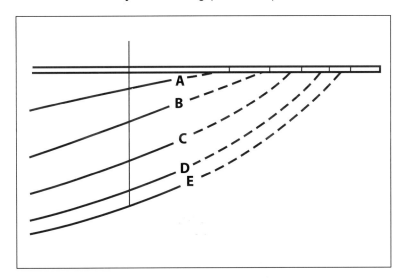

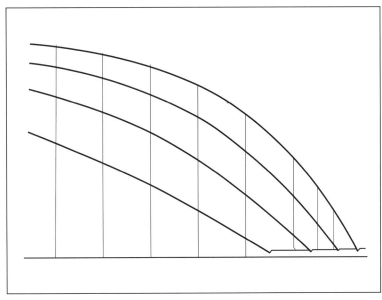

and stern; the rising line was essentially the same line viewed from the side rather than above. It became a purely theoretical concept towards the bow and stern as the main shape rose above the keel and had to be joined to it by straight or curved lines. The rising and narrowing lines of the breadth, however, were real throughout the length of the ship. The maximum breadth was higher in each successive frame towards the bow and stern, to help meet rough seas from behind or ahead. Continental shipwrights often used a device such as the Portuguese *graminho* to plan out the rising and narrowing lines by arithmetical means – a semicircle known as a *meia luna* or half moon, divided by parallel lines that could be measured off to produce a bevelled shape. But the men who built the *Mary Rose* may well have relied more on ribbands adjusted by eye.

The system had its faults. There is no evidence that the designers used 'waterlines' or horizontal sections through the underwater hull to improve the shape or 'fairing'. If they had done, they would have found a definite bulge at the lower level in the midships of the *Mary Rose*, which could have slightly reduced her sailing qualities; but in general it was a highly successful design.

Bow and stern

Books on shipbuilding were invariably silent about the vital areas of the bow and stern that were outside the master and quarter frame system, and whose shapes affected the

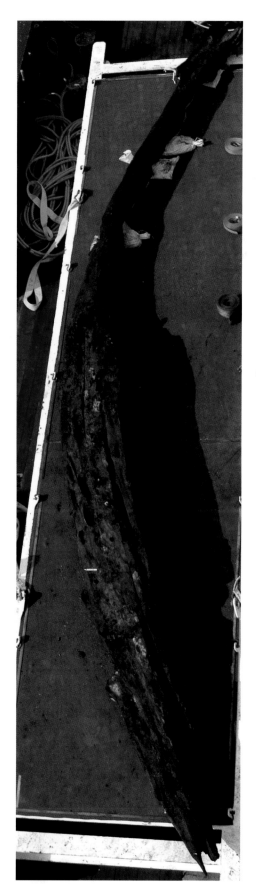

LEFT The curved stempost as recovered in 2005. This formed the core of the bow structure of the ship, and it allows a more accurate reconstruction of that area, although it is far from complete and the full shape of the bow will probably never be known for certain.

RIGHT AND BELOW Only a small part of the transom that formed the flat of the stern survives, as shown in the diagram. The rest of its shape had to be reconstructed from evidence such as the Anthony Roll as shown here. *(Pepys Library, Magdalene College, Cambridge)*

BELOW The waterlines towards the stern of the ship showing the fine 'run' towards the rudder, which allows it to operate in reasonably dense and stable water. The upper hull above the waterline at which the ship actually floats is much fuller, allowing the fitting of guns, cabins etc – although the stern of a ship of this period was always quite narrow.

PORT   STARBOARD

10

Section 12

6 Feet

5m

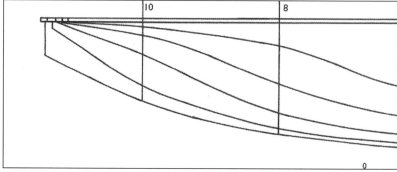

10   8

0

performance of the ship very much – perhaps this was the real secret of design, but if so it has not been revealed to us. A ship needed a bow that was sharp underwater, but bluff enough to meet the heaviest of seas, and which provided buoyancy to support the castles built above it, not to mention the heavy guns that would be added in increasing numbers. Practically nothing is known about the *Mary Rose*'s bow, apart from the stempost, which was recovered separately in 2005. No part of the starboard hull structure forward of this part has survived. The Anthony Anthony picture is unhelpful; like most ship pictures of the age it shows the stern rather than the bow, and in any case it gives no indication of the underwater shape. With a ship of a later generation we would expect the bow to be pointed at its lowest level, developing into a more rounded shape higher up, to support the guns mounted in the forecastle. Projections forward from the surviving frames suggest that

this was much less true of the *Mary Rose* and her contemporaries; the bow at the waterline was quite sharp. This was practicable because the guns intended to be carried in that area were lighter than those in the midships and stern. The lack of buoyancy in the area might help explain why the shipwrights were so reluctant to fit more armament in 1545, and why it was necessary to have forward-firing guns as far aft as the waist. It would have been difficult to design a bluffer bow using the system of battens, as they would have to be bent more sharply than was natural. They would be curved round from the foremost quarter frame to meet the stempost.

The upper shape of the rearmost part of the *Mary Rose* was formed by the flat shape of the stern. Only a fragment of it has survived, but it has the 10ft sweep or radius that was used in other parts of the ship. It was attached to the top of the sternpost, and in effect it was another

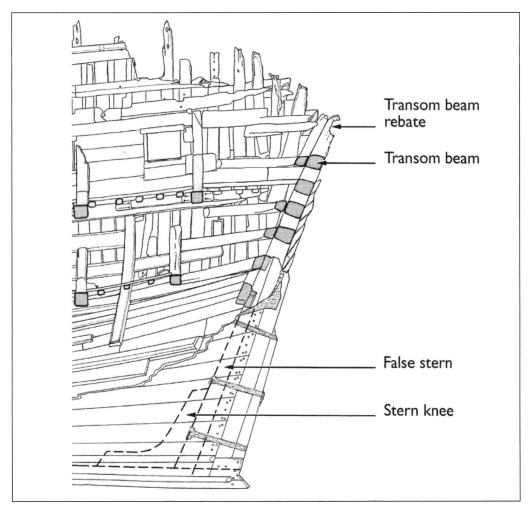

Transom beam rebate

Transom beam

False stern

Stern knee

LEFT Side view and section showing details of the stern structure. It is based on the angled sternpost, which receives the ends of the lower planking and supports several transoms that are fitted across the hull.

Cutaway of the hull of the *Mary Rose*.

(© Mary Rose Trust)

1 Bowsprit
2 Upper forecastle
3 Foremast
4 Lower forecastle
5 Structure raised in 1982
6 Soldiers
7 Archer
8 Upper deck
9 Sling
10 Gunners
11 Mainmast
12 Carpenter's cabin
13 Mizzen mast
14 Upper sterncastle deck
15 Ship's bell
16 Bonaventure mizzen

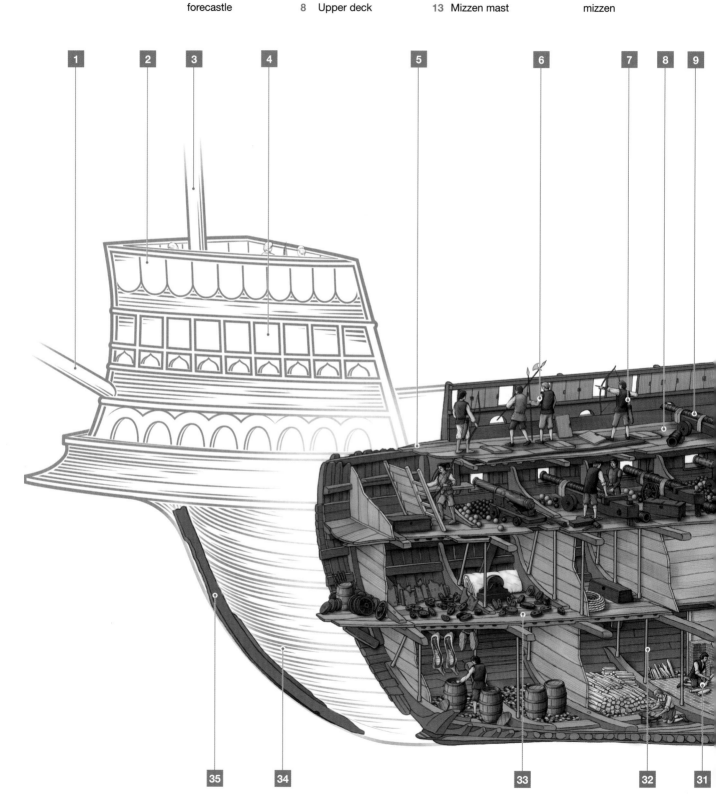

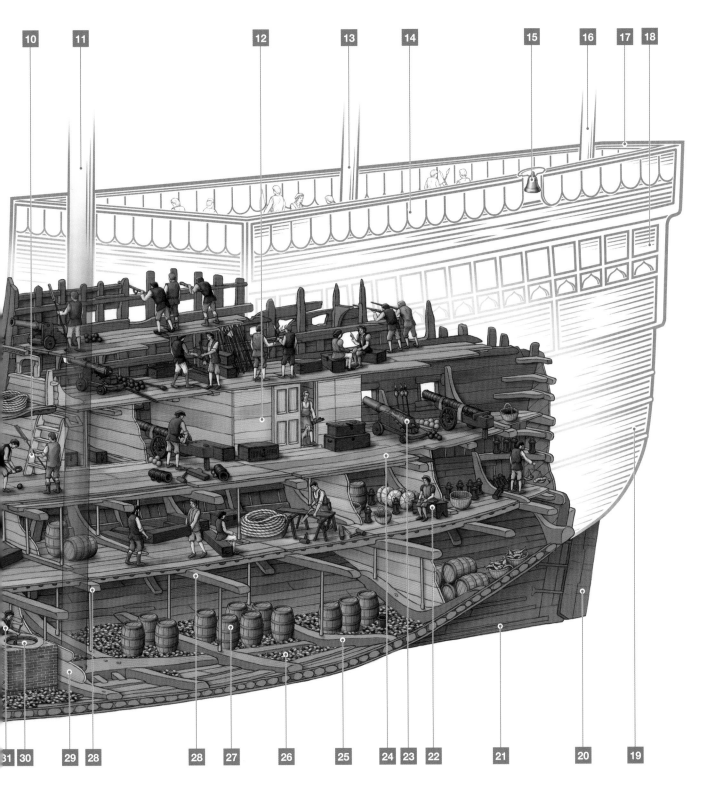

17	Sterncastle	21 Keel	26 Ballast	30 Cauldron	34 Bow
18	Lower sterncastle deck	22 Purser	27 Hold	31 Cooks	35 Curved stempost raised in 2005
19	Stern	23 Bronze cannon	28 Deck beams	32 Stanchion	
20	Rudder	24 Main deck	29 Mainmast step	33 Orlop deck	
		25 Rider			

quarter frame to which the ribbands could be attached. The underwater run had to be even finer in the stern than in the bows so that the rudder would not be in 'dead water', which would make the ship difficult to steer. Here we know more about the shape, and there was a distinctive hollow in the waterlines at the lower levels, with the hull tapering down to a very narrow section by about 10m forward of the rudder. But the after hull had to be much wider than the bow above the main waterline. Each frame in that area was V-shaped below, and increasingly sharp towards the rudder. Above that there was a concave curve, followed by a convex one that largely followed the system of sweeps as established by the master frame. These two curves formed the transition from the very narrow shape near the keel to the relatively broad one above water.

Construction

Even with extensive forests it was not possible to find timbers with the shape matching that of a whole ship's rib, so each individual frame was made in several overlapping sections. The lowest part, running across the keel, was the floor timber. In midships it was relatively flat and about 5m long. Towards the bow and stern each timber was successively more V-shaped. The floor timbers of the *Mary Rose* are irregular in size by later standards, varying from 200 to 495mm wide. They are very large, probably because the shipwrights were relatively new to carvel

construction and were cautious about it. Unlike the Mediterranean ships on which they were modelled, English ships often had to 'take the ground' or rest on a harbour bottom as the tide went out, and the effect of this was still largely unknown. Moreover, at that time there was no great shortage of timber to constrain the builders. The next sets of timbers were curved pieces known as futtocks, probably a corruption of 'foot-hook'.

Carvel building is often referred to as 'frame-first', as distinct from the 'skin-first', method of clinker. This is broadly true of ships of the *Mary Rose*'s period, but it does not mean that a complete frame was erected, then the planking put on. The most likely scenario is that the floor timbers of the master and quarter frames were fitted first. The next row of timbers consisted of the first futtocks, which curved upwards. They mainly touched the floor timbers and were sometimes joined to them by wooden pegs or trenails, so it seems possible that they were fixed at the same time, or soon afterwards. A keelson made of three oak timbers was fitted over the centres of the floor timbers, directly above the keel, to help lock the structure in place. The lower part of the bottom might well have been planked at this stage, then the next futtocks of the master and quarter frames installed. After that, ribbands were situated temporarily between them at successive levels and adjusted by eye to help shape the frames in between. Upper futtocks were added in good time to carry the shape up to the gunwales. The shipwright probably made 'moulds' or light

BELOW Some details of the floor timbers and riders as found in the recovered ship. Above them running from left to right, is the keelson that locks them in place, and a stout mast step is fitted over the keel.

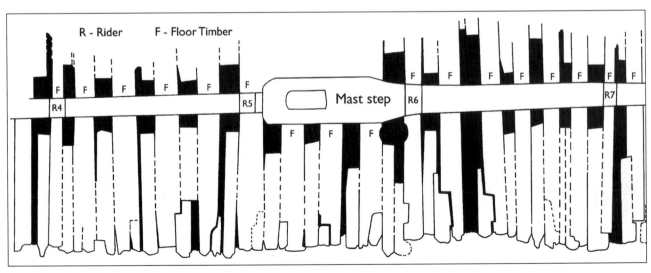

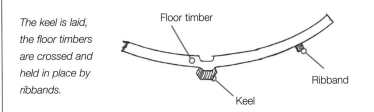

The keel is laid, the floor timbers are crossed and held in place by ribbands.

Floor timber

Ribband

Keel

ABOVE A trenail found in the wreck. Wooden fastenings were probably cheaper than metal in this period, they did not rust and their ends could be trimmed with the timbers and planks without damaging tools.

RIGHT Possible stages in the construction of the hull.

BELOW An iron nail from the wreck. This type of fastening was used in parts of the planking that did not need trimming, such as the decks.

The keelson is fitted to lock the floor timbers in position. The first futtocks are added and supported by ribbands. The lower battens are removed and the outer planking is fitted at the lowest level. Footwaling is added internally to strengthen the structure.

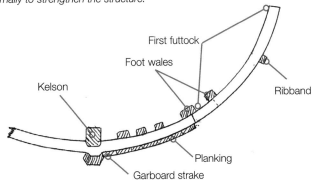

First futtock

Foot wales

Kelson

Ribband

Planking

Garboard strake

The second futtock is installed and held up by a ribband. The ceiling is fitted between the footwaling. The orlop deck clamp and beams are fitted.

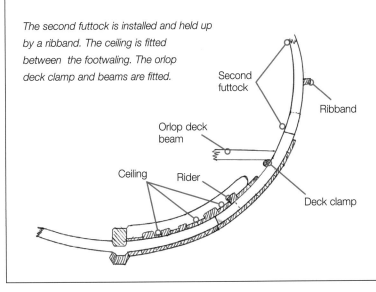

Second futtock

Ribband

Orlop deck beam

Ceiling

Rider

Deck clamp

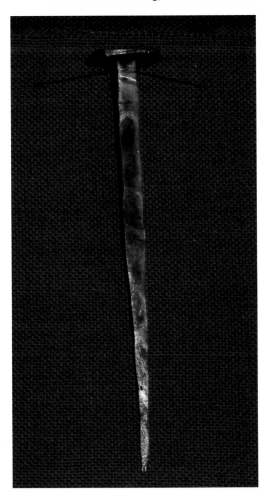

Bow

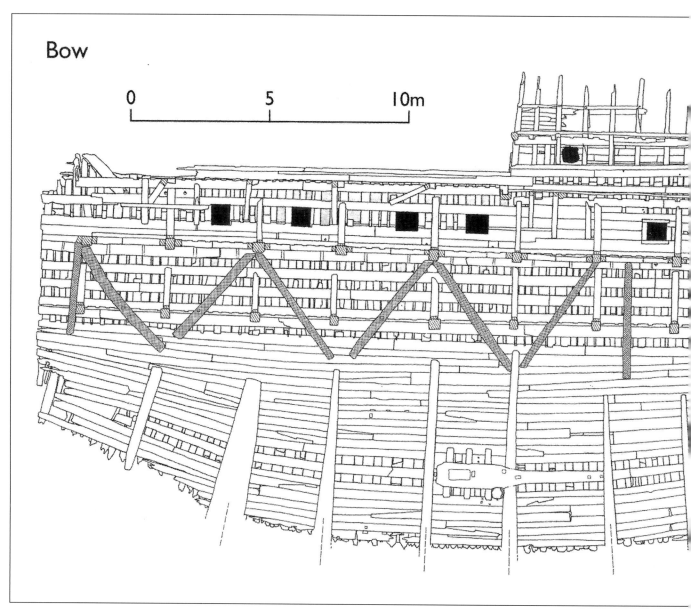

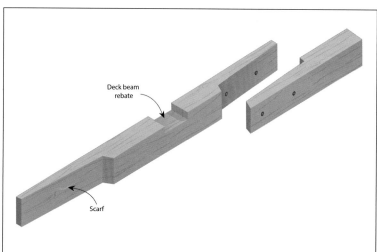

Deck beam rebate

Scarf

LEFT Plain scarfs in the clamp that was fitted inside the frames to support the deck beams, which in turn had their ends fixed into the rebate shown. *(John Lawson)*

BELOW A slightly more complex scarf joint, with 'tables' to prevent the timbers from it slipping up or down. *(John Lawson)*

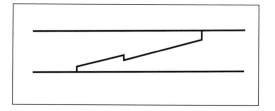

Stern

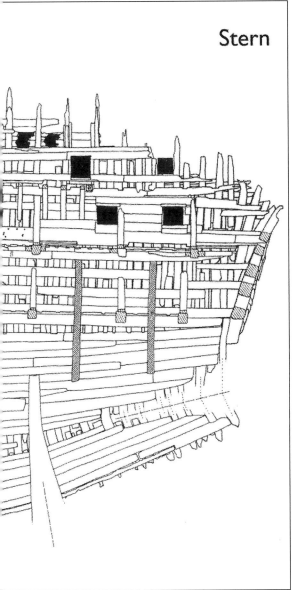

boards cut in the shape of repetitive frames, to take to the timber pile and find pieces that matched the size and grain of what he needed. Planking, internal as well as external, probably proceeded as soon as a suitable number of futtocks were in place, in order to lock the frames in position. Some of the futtocks were 'floating'; that is, they were not physically connected to neighbouring futtocks, so a system of ribbands followed by planking was essential.

Joining the timbers

Having cut the timbers to shape, the shipwrights had to join them in what they believed was an appropriate manner. When two pieces met at approximately right angles and crossed over one another, it was relatively simple to fasten them together. In the case of the carlings that were fitted between the deck beams, a rebate was cut in the larger piece to accommodate the smaller one. When a timber was intended to continue the line of the other, for example with the keel or to a certain extent with the timbers of the frame, it became more complex. The 'scarf' joint was one in which the ends of the two pieces overlapped, and were shaped this way to provide extra strength. Some were simple, with the pieces of each timber angled. Some were cut off at the end to form projections known as tables; others had two tables to lock the pieces together firmly against forces from either direction. Scarfs were used to bind the pieces of the keel and keelson, the stringers or footwaling of the internal

LEFT The inboard planking of the hull, with notches in 'dressmaker' style to show it as a flat surface. The shaded timbers are the braces that dendrochronology suggests were added late in the ship's life to improve her strength and help prevent hogging.

BELOW The carlines were lighter timbers that ran fore and aft between the pairs of deck beams. This diagram shows methods of joining the carlines to the deck beams as used on the *Mary Rose*. *(John Lawson)*

Carling

Deck beam

Carling

Deck beam

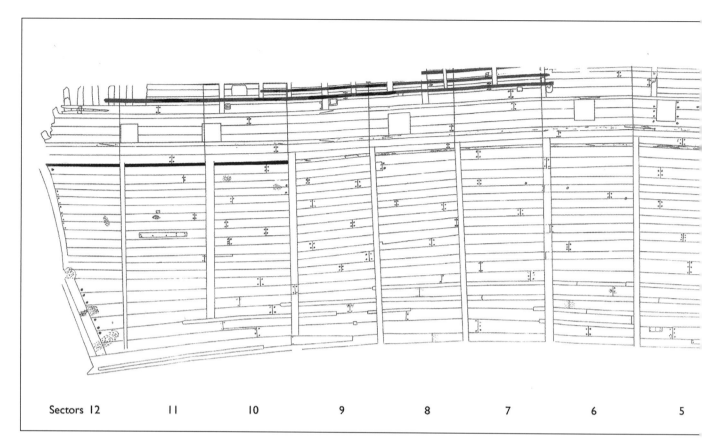

Sectors 12   11   10   9   8   7   6   5

ABOVE The outboard planking of the lower hull with the sternpost to the left. The joins of the strakes of rows of planking are shown as well as the areas obscured by the modern lifting frame.

planking, and the wales, the thicker part of the internal planking.

The standard method of connecting pieces of timber together was by means of trenails or 'tree-nails'. Each was a round wooden peg, often with a slight taper, which fitted in a hole

drilled in the pieces to be joined. It might be fixed in place using a wedge at one or both ends. Trenails were used for all the planking on the outside of the hull, with iron fastenings at the end of each plank to make sure they did not spring away from the hull. Iron bolts were

RIGHT A section through the centre of the hull showing the main features of the structure such as timbers, clamp, planking, beams and knees. The surviving parts are shaded and there is enough to give an almost complete picture of the structure at midships.
(John Lawson)

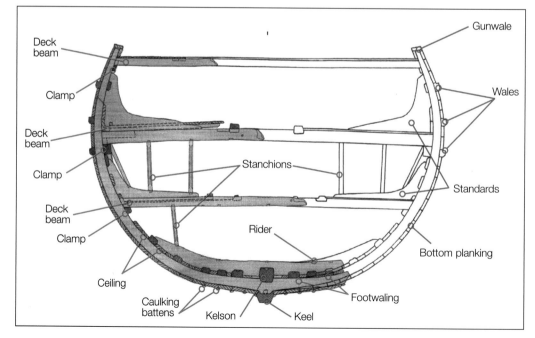

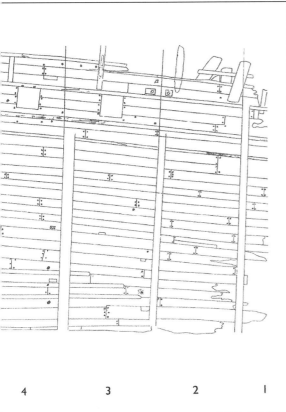

4   3   2   1

employed to fasten the keel scarfs and to fix knees in the hull, as well as braces, which were used to strengthen the hull during major repairs. Trenails had the advantage that wood did not rust, and that the shipwright could use his adze to trim the planking without fear of damaging his valuable tool.

Iron bolts were used where extra strength was needed and where the hull did not require trimming. Most plank ends had two iron bolts, and they were also used in knees. Some were 'blind' bolts that did not go all the way through; others were bolts that were probably fastened at the inner end by means of a hole in the bolt, a key that fitted through it and a washer; but nearly all of them rusted away during four centuries underwater, so it is difficult to be sure.

Planking

The internal planking of the lower hull (known as the ceiling although it was below rather than above the space in question) was probably fitted before the outer planking at this level, because it was more useful in locking the structure together. The thickest part consisted of planks known as footwales or stringers, which were placed above the joins between the floor timbers and the lower futtocks. Thinner planks were laid between them. There was a gap between the planking and the keelson to allow access; it was covered with removable planks known as limber boards.

The underwater external planking obviously needed a much smoother surface, and was around 4in thick in the lower part. It began with the 'garboard strake' next to the keel. Each row of planks, or 'strake', tended to taper towards the bow and stern, and some planks, known as 'stealers' ended before reaching the stem- or sternpost because the surface of the hull was less in these areas. Above the waterline a smooth surface was no longer necessary and thicker planks, known as 'wales', were fitted to give strength in the locality of the gunports, and perhaps to protect the hull when running alongside another ship in action. The wales were probably the first planks fitted in that area, with those around them tailored to fit. In the original design the hull was pierced with only two or three gunports on its lower deck, with five or six more cut out later. This involved interrupting the frame timbers, fitting a cill above

ABOVE A view of the upper outboard planking, showing many trenails. The remains of four iron fastenings at the butt join between planks can also be seen. The two bright bolts are modern titanium bolts retaining the hull in place.

and below the port, and ending the planking at the sides of each port.

Caulking was essential to keep the water out of the hull. A small gap was left between each two strakes of planking and filled with animal or vegetable fibre, often hair picked from cattle and formed into a loop. These were hammered into place by the caulker using his specialised tools, and covered with either pitch or tar made from pinewood. In the lower part of the hull the seams were often covered with long, thin battens nailed in place. The caulking had to be renewed constantly.

The upper works of the stern castle were planked in a very different style, the old-

fashioned clinker building with lighter and overlapping planks. These overlapping planks were also formed of cleft timber or by radial cutting rather than sawn planks, so the grain ran exactly up the plank. This made them very strong for their weight and also resistant to warping or splitting. That was important in an area of the ship that while at sea was alternately exposed to spray, sun, rain and wind.

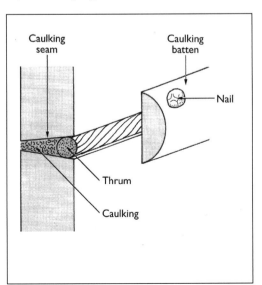

Caulking seam

Caulking batten

Nail

Thrum

Caulking

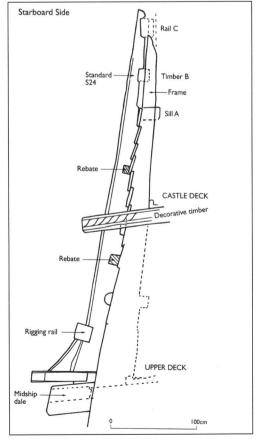

Starboard Side

Rail C

Standard S24

Timber B

Frame

Sill A

Rebate

CASTLE DECK

Decorative timber

Rebate

Rigging rail

UPPER DECK

Midship dale

0   100cm

LEFT The clinker construction of the stern castle with overlapping planks in an older style, and standards fitted outside for extra support.

FAR LEFT The method of caulking the lower hull. A smooth surface is not needed here as it would be underwater, so battens are used to cover the seams for extra protection.

RIGHT The
arrangements of the
decks of the ship
as recovered and
recorded are shown in
some detail here, while
the areas in the bow
and the upper stern
are projected with
dotted lines. Major
ships of the period
were to a certain
extent regarded as
'floating castles',
with sailing qualities,
and even stability,
sacrificed in order to
dominate opponents
both psychologically
and militarily.

Decks

The arrangement of the decks was fundamental to the concept of the ship. It might be possible to modify or rearrange some of the lighter decks in the fore- and after castles, but the other decks were an integral part of the structure. Their location affected many structural elements including the wales of the outer planking and most of the inner planking, as well as the siting of gunports. The term 'deck' was not always used in the modern sense in the early 16th century. It still retained its older meaning of a covering or roof, rather than the structure below on which one could walk. That was often known as the 'overlop' or 'orlop', which originally meant a narrow gangway, then a deck in current perception, and finally became restricted to the very lowest deck under the waterline – the terminology was very confused during the *Mary Rose*'s active lifetime.

The three major decks – which in modern terms are called the orlop, main deck and upper deck – were continuous throughout the length of the ship, which was probably more convenient than using split levels, but meant that they were very narrow, for example on the orlop near the bows. The upper deck had a step forward of the stern castle. The higher decks, towards the bow and stern, still showed some of their medieval origins in the temporary castles added to a merchant ship in wartime, although those of the *Mary Rose* were intended to be permanent. The main deck was divided into three key areas: the open waist in the centre and the sites under the castles at each end.

Above water, the system of internal planking was dominated by the needs of the decks. Thick planks known as clamps supported the deck beams from below. The other internal planking in this region was thinner, and positioned between the clamp and the deck below, with spaces cut for the gunports. Deck beams were probably fitted as soon as possible to keep the frames of the sides the correct distance apart, unless battens were used as a temporary measure. The decks had different functions and therefore slightly different systems of construction, but they had several features in common. The main strength was in

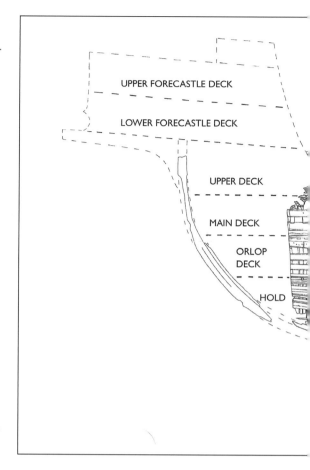

the stout beams, which were spaced regularly along the length of the ship running from side to side. Each beam was made in a single piece (except when it had been repaired using scarfs) and placed on top of the clamp. It was held in place by L-shaped knees, smaller ones known as hanging knees under the deck and larger ones, known as rising knees, above. The deck beams were linked by lighter timbers referred to as carlings, with their ends recessed into the beams. The carlings also formed the boundaries of features along the centre line of the ship, such as hatches and capstans.

The hold

At sea, the details of the construction of the hull were known only to the carpenters and caulkers who had to maintain them. The other features of the ship, deck by deck, were better known to the officers, sailors, gunners and soldiers on board. Certainly the deck features would be very familiar if only because of the numerous hazards – low beams to bang one's head on, knees to trip over and hatches to fall down were all threats to the

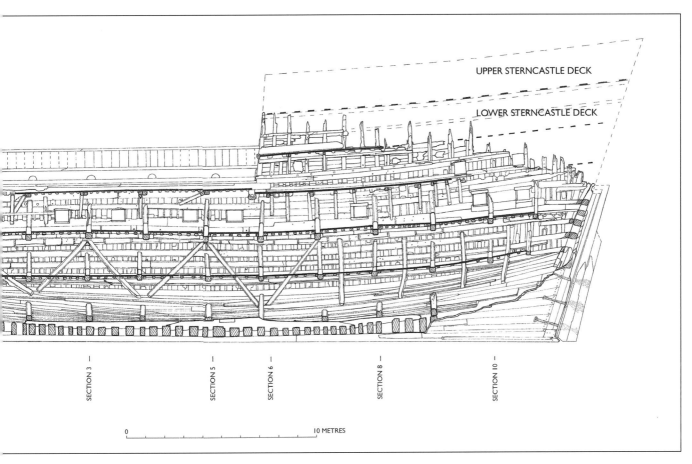

UPPER STERNCASTLE DECK

LOWER STERNCASTLE DECK

SECTION 3

SECTION 5

SECTION 6

SECTION 8

SECTION 10

0   10 METRES

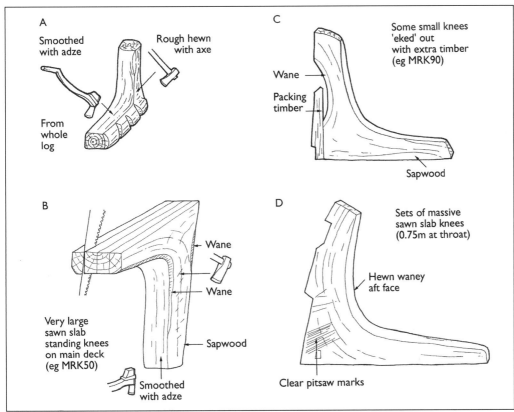

A

Smoothed
with adze

Rough hewn
with axe

From
whole
log

B

Wane

Wane

Very large
sawn slab
standing knees
on main deck
(eg MRK50)

Sapwood

Smoothed
with adze

C

Some small knees
'eked' out
with extra timber
(eg MRK90)

Wane

Packing
timber

Sapwood

D

Sets of massive
sawn slab knees
(0.75m at throat)

Hewn waney
aft face

Clear pitsaw marks

LEFT The methods for
making knees. These
were key structural
elements to prevent
the hull from racking,
and ideally they should
be made from carefully
chosen timber. That
was not always
available, or some
of them decayed in
service so they had to
be eked out.

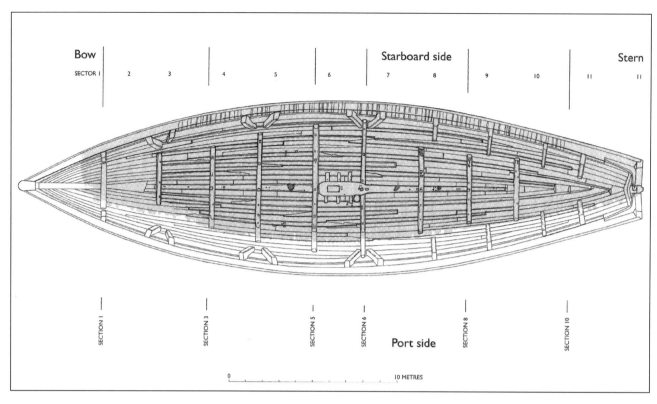

Bow   Starboard side   Stern

SECTOR 1   2   3   4   5   6   7   8   9   10   11   11

SECTION 1   SECTION 3   SECTION 5   SECTION 6   SECTION 8   SECTION 10

Port side

0   10 METRES

ABOVE The plan of the hold, which is almost complete in the wreck apart from the bow and some of the port side. The keelson runs along the centre with the mainmast step in midships. The riders in the hold are also indicated. Surviving parts are shaded

unwary sailor, and even more the soldier who was not so used to such an environment.

The hold was the lowest part of the interior, its shape determined by the need to provide good lines for sailing. It was less familiar to the crew, except the cooks who worked in the galley there and the sailors who might be sent down to retrieve goods from the storage areas. Its lowest level was formed by the ceiling above the frame timbers, and that was surmounted by nine riders, heavy timbers that followed the shape of the floor and gave extra

reinforcement. Right in the centre was the step of the mainmast, set above the keel and with a large rectangular rebate to accommodate the heel of the mast. For most of the time this was covered with flint ballast, which was probably taken from beaches in Portsmouth and Langstone Harbours. This performed two functions – to weight the lower part of the hull to help it to stay upright in the wind, and to provide a level surface for stowing the casks in the hold. Staved wooden casks (popularly known as barrels) have been found in the wreck

RIGHT Views of the hold and the orlop deck above it. The floor timbers are shown sectioned in this diagram, with the riders above them. The orlop deck is relatively light as it does not have to support guns.

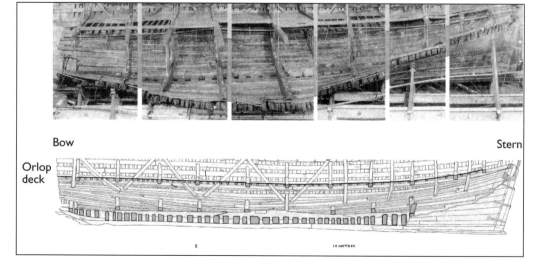

Bow   Stern

Orlop deck

0   10 METRES

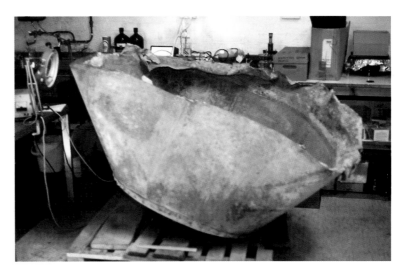

ABOVE A cask found in the ship. Its willow hoops are missing but its staves can be reconstructed. Casks of various types were the standard means of storing food, drink and gunpowder.

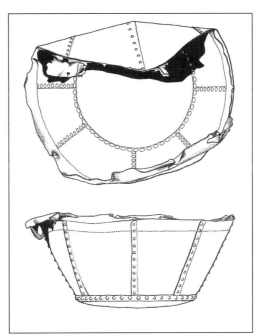

LEFT A drawing of the cauldron or copper kettle, with its rim made of lead.

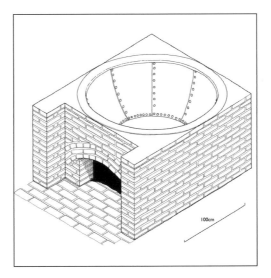

LEFT A reconstruction of the brick firehearth that held the cauldron, showing the furnace underneath. It presented an obvious risk on board a wooden ship and the fire was put out if action threatened. The crew's provisions were usually boiled, although officers perhaps had a more sophisticated cuisine.

of the *Mary Rose*, containing victuals such as beef, pork, fish and fruit, or wine. One, filled with pork, was hanging over the starboard side, perhaps to form part of the next day's meal. Others held stores such as pitch, candles and tallow. The food and water casks were probably arranged in two or three tiers in the hold, interlocked with one another and possibly held in place by wedges.

The hold also contained the galley where the crew's food was cooked. The position was well away from gunfire and other hazards; its low situation aided the ship's stability and it was close to where the food was stored, but it must have created other problems. It was a difficult space to ventilate and keep cool, or to let smoke escape, while there was a constant danger of fire spreading. The galley was placed just forward of midships in the hold – it was a heavy area that was best placed near the centre of the ship for stability, but it had to avoid the

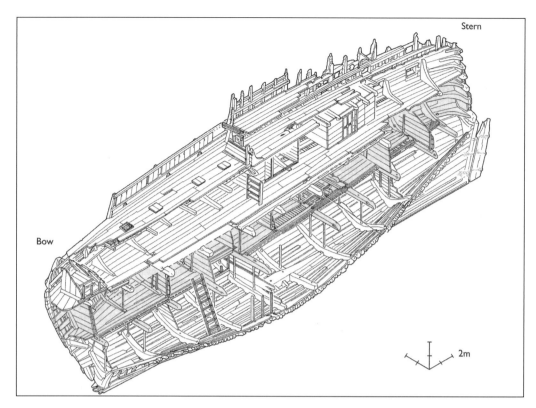

Stern

Bow

2m

mainmast. The galley, described in the records as 'great copper kettles in furnace set in lime and brick closed above with lead', consisted of two brick furnaces side by side, each with a deep circular copper pan or cauldron. The whole location was enclosed in a wooden partition.

The orlop deck

The lowest deck, known in modern terminology as the orlop deck, was below the waterline and could not be expected to carry guns. It was comparatively light in construction, supported by timber known as clamp and averaging about 110mm by 140mm in cross section, which supported 11 evenly spaced beams around 300mm by 285mm in section. There was a row of carlines between them running fore and aft, with a wider gap in the centre line above the galley furnace. Lighter pieces known as half beams ran between the carlines, parallel to the beams. There were short pieces of plank amid these knees, and longer pieces further inboard. The central part of the deck, inboard of the row of carlines, was taken up with hatchways covered with wooden covers, allowing access to the stores in the hold.

The orlop deck contained one of the most intriguing features of the *Mary Rose*. Bracing timbers ran diagonally and vertically across the inner structure. The diagonals, in particular, provided an answer to the greatest weakness of carvel building. Unlike clinker building the planks were not joined to one another, so the whole hull may well have flexed as it got older. All the diagonal braces that have been studied by dendrochronology have been shown to date from a rebuild in the 1530s, suggesting they were added to the hull then to reduce this. There is no evidence on how successful they were in helping the ship keep its shape, but the idea was evidently not followed up in future ships. It recurred several times over the next three centuries, until Robert Seppings made it standard for the Royal Navy in 1811.

The deck was divided into at least eight or nine compartments by wooden partitions attached to one side of most of the knees. They may have been accessed through the hatches above. They contained various goods, including three anchor cables, gunnery equipment, spare pieces of rigging, galley stores including firewood and tableware, casks of food and some personal possessions. Either they were stored there out of the way, or the area provided a certain amount of crew accommodation.

The main deck

The main deck was the first level above the waterline. While it only carried a limited number of heavy guns in its early days, its beams were around 300 to 400mm square, making them more than 40% stronger than the orlop deck beams. In addition, they were strongly supported by lodging knees flush with

LEFT Upper deck hatches.

the deck and rising knees above – these were very long on their lower end, and would have created an extra trip hazard for the unwary soldier or sailor. There was a single row of carlings, although this was doubled up in midships with an extra row almost touching the main one. The deck was planked with 70mm oak, which varied quite considerably in width and length, perhaps because of repair. It was fitted with openings known as scuppers to allow water to drain out. In its final form the deck was cut for at least seven square gunports on the starboard side, irregularly

BELOW The structure on the starboard side between the main and upper decks, showing gunports, knees, standards and planking. The beams of the main deck are the heaviest as they have to support many of the guns. The arrangement of the gunports is irregular.

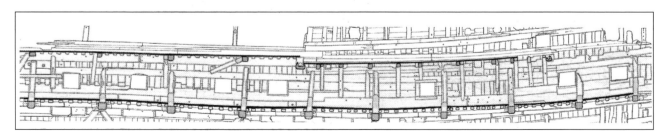

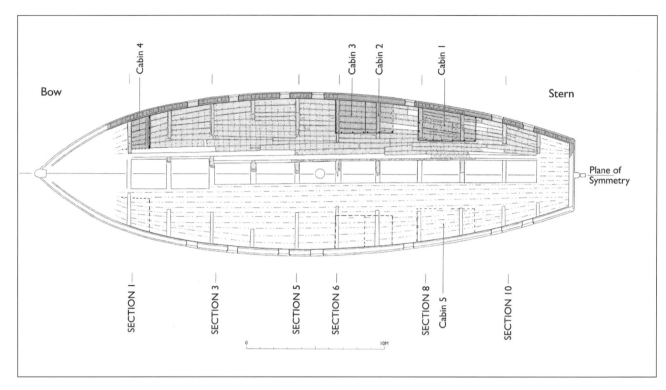

Cabin 4

Cabin 3
Cabin 2

Cabin 1

Bow

Stern

Plane of
Symmetry

SECTION 1

SECTION 3

SECTION 5

SECTION 6

SECTION 8
Cabin 5

SECTION 10

0   10M

spaced and with the arc of fire often restricted
by rising knees. Each was fitted with a port lid
that could be closed to keep out enemy shot,
or water in rough seas or when heeling – a
crucial point, as it turned out, on the ship's
final voyage. The drawings in the Anthony Roll
suggest that the *Mary Rose*, like most ships
of the period, also had two ports in the stern

where heavy guns could be mounted – none
were recovered from this position during the
20th-century excavation, perhaps because
they had been salvaged earlier.

The gunports were quite small by later
standards, typically about 700mm wide and
600mm high, so there was not much room to
elevate or traverse a gun that might be about

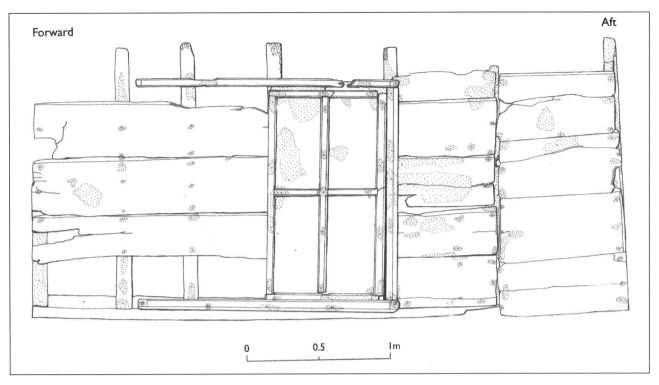

0   0.5   1m

400mm in diameter at that point. Each was cut between two of the main futtock timbers, with another timber interrupted by the port. The head and foot of the port were mostly formed by cills, pieces of wood fitted between the futtocks. Each of the main deck ports had a lid that was hinged above. There was a ring bolt on the inside, and it is not fully established how

the ports were opened. Presumably the gun crew pushed each port lid open with bars from the side, while another team hauled on it from the deck above.

As further proof that gunnery was not yet the main function of a warship and it was not considered essential to site as many guns as possible on the lower deck, the area

ABOVE The carpenter's cabin on the main deck, with its sliding door. At some stage in the life of the ship, the carpenter had extended the cabin by 900mm, which is why the partition planking on the right is in a different style.

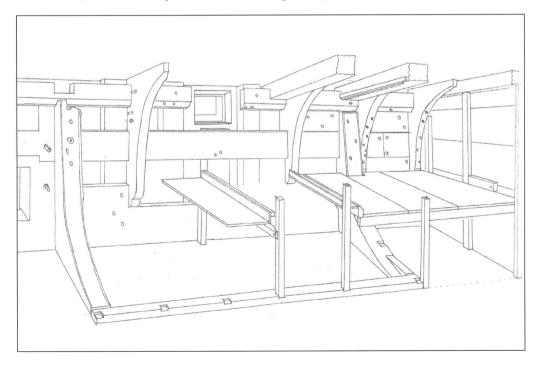

LEFT The interior of the cabin, probably used by the carpenter and his crew as a storeroom as well as living quarters, so that tools and materials could be stored with a certain amount of security from theft.

RIGHT The step in the upper deck at the forward end of the stern castle, including a knee that supported the forward face of the castle structure.

BELOW Possible reconstruction of the roof structure that supported netting during battle. It was intended to protect the ship from boarders, but had the unfortunate effect of trapping many of the crew when the ship capsized.

was also fitted with several cabins near the stern, built permanently in wood and clearly not removable for action. The largest single one on the starboard side was used by the carpenter and his team, not just for living in but as a storeroom. Forward of that was one for the surgeon, judging by the stores found in it. There was another cabin well forward on the starboard side, once known as the pilot's cabin because it contained navigational instruments, although it was well away from a pilot's normal work station near the stern. No cabins were found on the missing port side, but surviving chests indicate they may have been fitted. Logic would suggest that the boatswain would have one in that area, equal in status to that of the carpenter.

The upper deck

The upper deck was also continuous along the length of the ship, and it was the first one to be open to the elements, in the central area known as the waist. The beams were not quite as strong as those of the main deck, averaging 260mm by 230mm, for it was intended to carry lighter guns. Unlike the main deck it

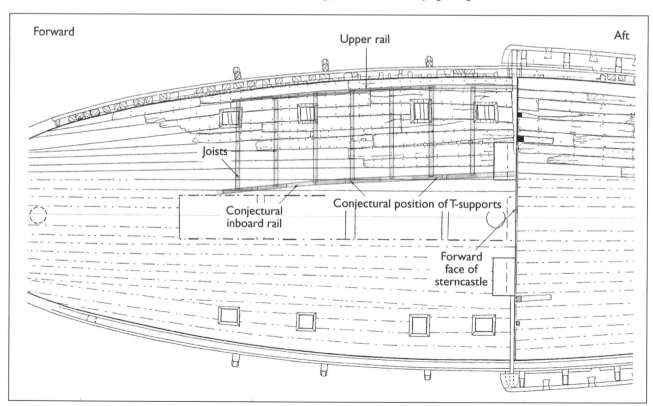

Forward — Aft

Upper rail

Joists

Conjectural inboard rail

Conjectural position of T-supports

Forward face of sterncastle

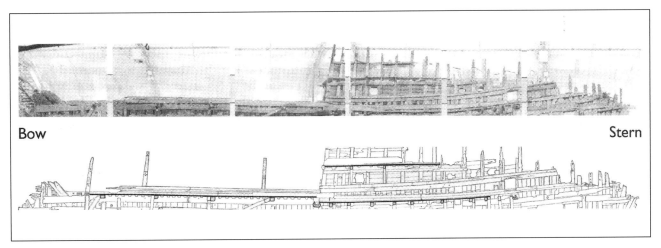

Bow

Stern

was not punctuated by rising knees, perhaps because it had to be kept clear to allow the sailors to handle ropes and sails. Instead, it was supported from underneath by hanging knees. The deck was interrupted at the forward end of the aftercastle, and rises about 270mm at that point. The space under the stern castle was largely for accommodation, although chests of longbows and large numbers of pikes and bills were found there. Perhaps they had fallen from the deck above, or the area served as a muster station for archers and soldiers. The waist was mainly a fighting and working area. As such it was fitted with three very low, small, semicircular gunports plus two substantial rectangular ports in the stern. Above those in the waist are the 'blinds', light panels that helped shelter archers, with alternate ones removable in action. The waist had a roof or gangway down its centre line supported by T-shaped timbers. These helped to hold a netting over the area, which was erected as a precaution against boarding but had fatal effects in July 1545.

The remains of eight to ten chests were found under the stern castle. Some contained weapons such as longbows, which had probably been brought up ready for action, some had navigational equipment such as compass and dividers, but others held personal belongings, confirming that the area was used for accommodation – although very little of the rearmost part, where the senior officers might have lived, has survived. There is even less of the upper deck forward of the waist, under the forecastle, but its deck seems to be continuous with the waist.

The castles

Little survives of the after- or stern castle on the *Mary Rose*, although it is clear that much of its sides were made in clinker rather than carvel built. Documentary evidence suggests that there were two decks in the aftercastle, probably called the 'middle deck' and 'upper deck' or 'high deck' by contemporaries. A little of the lower of these two decks survives, and its structure can largely be determined by the clamp that supported it, showing space for 11 or 12 deck beams. The higher deck does not survive, but it is shown in the Anthony Roll as having equal length with the lower one, and surmounted by a netting similar to the one in the waist. The lower aftercastle deck was apparently fitted for light guns. Both came to an end with a strong wooden bulkhead known as the 'barbican head'. By 1545 it was pierced for two forward-firing medium-sized guns at the lower level, and two more on the upper deck.

Practically nothing survives of the forecastle, and no physical evidence exists of a castle deck that was believed to be above it, but this is one of the most intriguing parts of the ship. It seems to have been comparatively light in structure and may well have been triangular in plan, or at least with a very narrow forward face. This, and the relatively small amount of buoyancy created by the underwater hull, made it very difficult to fit forward-firing guns. It also had two decks. The bulkhead of its after face sloped forward, which is seen with perhaps some exaggeration in the illustration in the Anthony Roll, and partly confirmed by archaeology. The picture also shows a smaller structure on the aftermost part of the uppermost deck.

ABOVE The structure on the starboard side of the upper deck, showing the surviving sides of the stern castle. Unfortunately, the counterpart in the bows has not survived so very little is known about it, although it was probably regarded as a crucial area in fighting the ship.

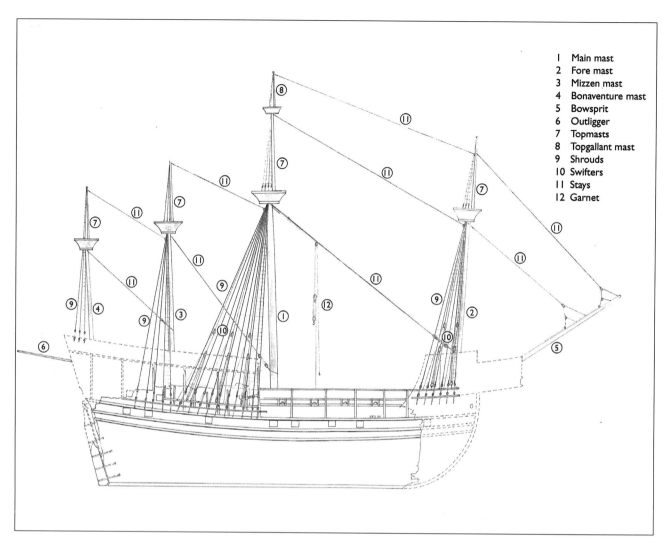

1	Main mast
2	Fore mast
3	Mizzen mast
4	Bonaventure mast
5	Bowsprit
6	Outligger
7	Topmasts
8	Topgallant mast
9	Shrouds
10	Swifters
11	Stays
12	Garnet

ABOVE The suggested arrangement of masts, yards and standing rigging, not to scale. The four-masted rig, with the small bonaventure mizzen right at the after end, was common for large ships at the time. The shrouds that supported the masts from the sides and aft are shown prominently, with the less obvious stays running diagonally forward from the masts.

Masts

The most prominent feature of any sailing ship is its masts and rigging, although very little of them have survived and we are reliant on documentary evidence, the Anthony Roll and comparison with other ship pictures of the period. The details of the rigging would be very familiar to the sailors on board, but far less so to the gunners and soldiers, even though some of them might have to help haul on ropes when needed.

The *Mary Rose* had four masts plus a bowsprit that projected at an angle from the bow, as was common for larger ships of the day. The mainmast, part of which was recovered by John Deane in 1840, was fitted near the centre of the ship with its lower end 'stepped above the keelson in midships'. The surviving portion was about 15ft long and was described

rather vaguely as 'nearly as large as that of a 75-gun ship'. If this meant the standard 74-gun ship of the day, then it was nearly 37in or 0.94m in diameter; but unlike a large mast of 1840 it was made in a single piece, suggesting that suitable timber was not in short supply. Its height can only be guessed at, with about 7.4m below decks and perhaps 18m above the upper deck in the waist. The foremast was fitted well forward and barely within the main structure of the hull if the Anthony Roll is to be believed. It was presumably stepped on the stempost, although nothing showing its fitting has survived. It was shorter than the mainmast, with its head on a slightly lower level than that of the mainmast. The two aftermasts were considerably lighter. The mizzen was probably fitted about the middle of the aftercastle. The bonaventure mast was about as far aft as the foremast was forward.

A 'top' was fitted at the head of each lower

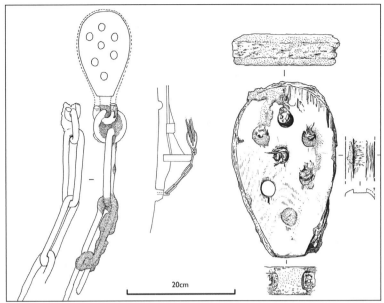

mast. Until quite recently it had been known as the topcastle, another platform (like the forecastle and aftercastle) from which darts and arrows could be projected towards the enemy. A small top survives from the *Mary Rose*, presumably kept as a spare on the orlop deck. It is circular and bowl-shaped as shown in many paintings and drawings of the period, but very small, with a diameter of 1.45m, so presumably it was used for one of the upper masts. It still served as a fighting platform, but also as a means to spread the rigging of the

topmast, and a base for men or boys working on the yards.

Standing rigging

No mast was strong enough to carry sail and resist the forces of the wind on its own, and each needed a good deal of rope to support it. This was known as the standing rigging of the ship, as it did not have to be adjusted during manoeuvres, but only for maintenance purposes. From behind and the sides, each mast had several thick ropes known as shrouds

ABOVE AND ABOVE LEFT A lower deadeye showing the means of attaching it to the hull with chains. Rope lanyards ran between each pair of deadeyes and passed through the holes. They were used to tighten the shrouds, as they tended to stretch in service.

LEFT A selection of rigging blocks and other rigging items, including metal sheaves and part of a parrel that held the yard against the mast.

running diagonally downwards and aft from the masthead. According to the inventory of 1514, she had 13 shrouds per side on the mainmast, 8 on the foremast, 6 on the mizzen and 4 on the bonaventure mizzen. The upper ends were looped round the masthead, with the lower ends attached to heart-shaped blocks known as 'deadmen's eyes' or later as deadeyes. Each of these was linked to a lower deadeye by ropes known as lanyards; they were spread by projections from the side of the hull known as 'chain wales' or channels, and underneath that they were joined to the side of the ship by chains. Each set of shrouds had much lighter ropes known as ratlines running horizontally between them to provide a ladderway for the crew to ascend. Thick ropes known as stays ran diagonally forward and downward from each mast to hold it if the wind came from ahead, either during tacking or due to a sudden shift. They were fixed on deck, except for the fore shroud, which led to the bowsprit.

BELOW
Reconstruction of the yards of the ship. The fore and aft yards, running diagonally in this drawing, are shown in almost their natural position. The square yards, running horizontally, are set parallel to the centre line of the ship to show their length (but cut short in this illustration), although they would not be able to reach such a position in real life.

The other masts

It was only in the last few decades before the *Mary Rose* was built, almost within living memory then, that a mast had been expected to carry more than one sail. The upper mast, now known as the topmast, had developed quite recently from a glorified flagpole to a true mast with shrouds, stays and other rigging all of its own. Each of the four masts had a topmast that began from a hole in the top, and the main topmast had a small topgallant mast above that. The main topmast had five shrouds per side, the topgallant had three and the bonaventure mizzen had four. Each had its own stay, usually leading diagonally forward to a point on the mast ahead, and to the bowsprit in the case of the fore topmast stay.

Very little is known about the bowsprit, which projected forward of the bow at an angle of perhaps 40°. As well as providing an anchorage for the stays of the foremast and fore topmast, it still served its original function,

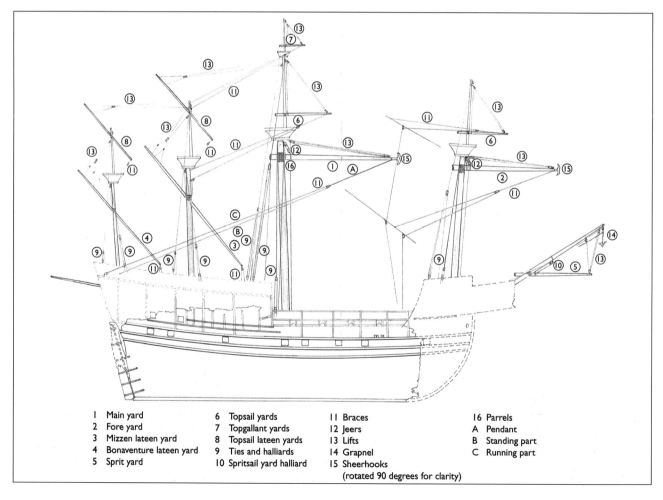

I	Main yard	6	Topsail yards	I I	Braces	16	Parrels
2	Fore yard	7	Topgallant yards	12	Jeers	A	Pendant
3	Mizzen lateen yard	8	Topsail lateen yards	13	Lifts	B	Standing part
4	Bonaventure lateen yard	9	Ties and halliards	14	Grapnel	C	Running part
5	Sprit yard	10	Spritsail yard halliard	15	Sheerhooks		
					(rotated 90 degrees for clarity)		

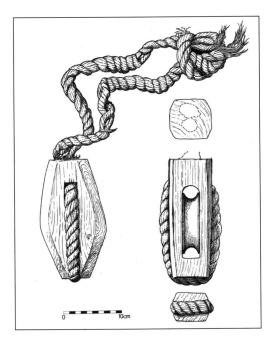

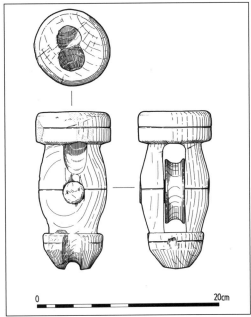

FAR LEFT A block with its rope still attached. The sheave, seen in the centre of the right-hand drawing, is circular and rotates with the rope that is passing through it. It might be used to alter the direction of the rope, perhaps allowing it to be controlled from the deck.

LEFT An unusual type of block with a projection round its head (its exact purpose has not been established and blocks of this type have not been found on other ships) but it is possibly a clew garnet block used to haul up the lower corner of a sail.

to haul on the bowlines that held the edges of the foresail forward when sailing close to the wind. A small sail known as the spritsail could also be hung under it.

Yards and their rigging

Each of the yards carried its own sail. The foresail, fore topsail, mainsail, main topsail, main topgallant and spritsail were all square sails – not because of their shape, as only the main-, fore- and spritsails were rectangular, but because in their neutral position they were at right angles, or square to the keel of the ship. There is no detailed information on their lengths, but it can be surmised that the main yard, which spread the top of that sail, was slightly longer than the ship was wide, that is about 12m, and the other yards were in proportion. The other spars – the mizzen, mizzen topsail and bonaventure – were lateen yards, from 'Latin', implying their Mediterranean origin. They carried triangular sails, and each yard was normally set at about 45° to the vertical, with part of the sail forward of the mast.

The yards, especially the fore and main, were supported by a surprisingly complex systems of ropes and blocks. They could be raised by two alternative, or complementary, methods. The tie was a rope fitted to the centre of the yard and led through a sheave set in a hole near the head of the mast. The tie passed downwards aft of the mast to be linked to the halyard ('haul-

yard') through a pair of blocks, then secured to a timber known as the knight's head on deck. The second method used the jeer blocks, which were probably attached on either side of the centre of the yard, and used in conjunction with another pair of blocks under the top. The other yards only used the ties and halyards, but in each case the yard was secured against the mast by means of a complex but elegant system of balls or trucks and ribs joined by rope and known collectively as parrels. The rope could be loosened to allow the yard to slide up or down, or perhaps to operate some distance from the mast, and was tightened when it was fixed in place. The yard was kept level (or at a different angle when required) by means of ropes known as lifts attached to the ends and led back to the masthead. The angle with the wind was crucial in sailing, and that was controlled by the braces, one leading from the end of each yard.

LEFT A double block with two sheaves side by side – a common type on most ships and used in various sizes in a block and tackle arrangement to lift heavy weights including spars, guns and provisions.

Chapter Three

The crew

Without the study of what was found in the *Mary Rose,* we would know very little about Tudor sailors and soldiers apart from admirals and captains. The clothing, skeletons and personal items reveal much about the people and their daily lives on board.

OPPOSITE One gallon of ale was allocated per day for each crew member due to the difficulty of storing water onboard. The remains of 17 relatively complete wooden drinking tankards have been recovered. *(Courtesy Stephen Foote)*

Captains

A naval commander, whether admiral or captain, was not a seaman in those days. He was usually a soldier of aristocratic origin, who had spent at least as much time on land as sea warfare. One was appointed only when the ship was ready for sea and about to go to war. The *Mary Rose*'s first commander was Sir Edward Howard, younger son of the Earl of Surrey, who had been restored to royal favour despite fighting on the losing side against Henry VII at the Battle of Bosworth in 1485. He was a skilled jouster, which won the approval of Henry VIII, and he and his elder brother Thomas took part in a seafaring exploit that killed the Scottish adventurer Andrew Barton in 1511. In April 1512 at the age of about 35 Edward was appointed to command the fleet from the *Mary Rose*, and he sailed in her until his death in action at Blanc-Sablon in April 1513. He was an innovative but dangerously impetuous commander. The distinction between the admiral and the flag captain was not clear in those days, but Howard's cousin Sir Thomas Wyndham served under him and perhaps fulfilled the latter role. When Howard was killed, his elder brother Thomas took over as admiral before playing a prominent part in the defeat of the Scottish army at Flodden. He had Edward Bray, the nephew of the king's minister Sir Reginald Bray, as his assistant. Thomas Howard remained with the *Mary Rose* for the rest of that war, and sailed in her again during the next one, which began in 1522. He was described as 'small and spare in person, his hair black'. He was sociable and ambitious, and climbed the greasy pole of Tudor politics until he was accused of treason, only avoiding execution because of the king's death in 1547.

In 1545 Sir George Carew was appointed to the *Mary Rose* for a new war. He was around 40, the son of a Devon landowner, and he too had much experience of politics and warfare. He was a member of the House of Commons and served with the army in France. He also had sea experience, patrolling against pirates in 1537 and helping to escort Anne of Cleves to England two years later. From 1543 he was a lieutenant general of horse in the campaign in Flanders before being designated to the *Mary Rose*. Though she was old by this time, there were still few ships bigger than her and she became a flagship again when Henry personally bestowed Carew with the gold whistle and chain of a vice-admiral.

Masters

The officer who conducted the sailing of the ship was the master, usually of much humbler birth than the captain or admiral. The *Mary Rose*'s master for her fitting out was John Clerke. During most of her early years the post was held by Thomas Sperte, whose origins are typically obscure for a man of that station. He first comes to notice as master of the *Mary Rose* from 1511, and then for recruiting mariners from his base at Stepney on the Thames near London. He travelled to the king's palace at Eltham to advise on keeping ships during the winter, and had a budget of £200 to look after her during 1512–13. He was also an expert pilot, and was paid for 'lodesmanshippe' on a voyage to Danzig, and for conducting the *Mary Rose* in the Thames. He was an

OPPOSITE **Sir Thomas Howard who became Lord High Admiral at the age of 35 in 1512 and led the fleet from the *Mary Rose*, as seen in a 1539 portrait by Holbein.** *(Royal Collection Trust/© Her Majesty Queen Elizabeth II 2015)*

BELOW **Sir George Carew, who came from a prominent Devon family and served the king by land and sea before he commanded the ship in 1545 and was lost when she sank. By Hans Holbein the Younger.** *(Royal Collection Trust/ © Her Majesty Queen Elizabeth II 2015)*

S G Carow Knight

able man, promoted to master of the new *Henri Grace à Dieu* in 1513, and carrying out various administrative tasks. Although the post of master was an important one, it is not clear who succeeded to it after that.

According to William Bourne in 1574, a master,

> *… ought to be sober and wise, and not to be light or rash-headed, nor to be fumish and hasty, but such a one as can well govern himself, for else it is not possible for him to govern his company well: he ought not to be simple, but he must be such a one as must keep his company in awe of him (by discretion) doing his company no injury or wrong. … And the Principal point in government is, to cause himself both to be feared and loved. …*

In a nautical scene described in the *Complaint of Scotland* of 1549, the master was in complete charge as the ship raised anchor and set sail. He used his whistle and voice to send men up to loose the sails, to set a bonnet and set the topsails. He directed the helmsman to steer 'full and by', a boy to the top to shake out the flag on the topmast, as well as a host of other orders.

The specialists

The purser was the supply officer of the ship, with the thankless task of providing food and drink when the supply system was deeply flawed. In 1523 the deficiencies of the shore organisation did not stop the pursers being collectively accused of 'an outrageous lack' for which they deserved hanging. Formally the purser was roughly equal in status to the boatswain, perhaps slightly superior. We know the names of some of the holders of the office in the *Mary Rose*: David Boner in 1511, John Lawden in 1512–13 and John Brerely later in that year.

Surgeons were considerably inferior to physicians in those days, for they had trained by apprenticeship rather than in university. They were still linked with barbers as wielders of sharp instruments, and indeed in London the Fellowship of Surgeons merged with the Barbers' Guild in 1540 – the barbers gained by association with a slightly superior class of tradesman, while the surgeons gained entry to a city livery company, with all its powers and privileges. King Henry himself was happy to be painted by Holbein with the members of the company. The association between barbers and surgeons, and their practice of bleeding

RIGHT This picture was reconstructed from the remains of a man found on the orlop deck, believed to be the *Mary Rose*'s purser. He was with a chest containing gold and silver coins, for he was responsible for paying the crew and finding supplies. *(The Mary Rose Trust/ Oscar Nilsson)*

FAR RIGHT The cook served under the purser and was paid the same as the master carpenter and the master gunner. He was responsible for feeding over 400 men. An inscription on a bowl and tankard suggest that his name was a variation of Ny Cop or Ny Coep. *(The Mary Rose Trust/ Oscar Nilsson)*

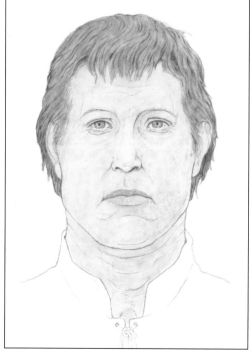

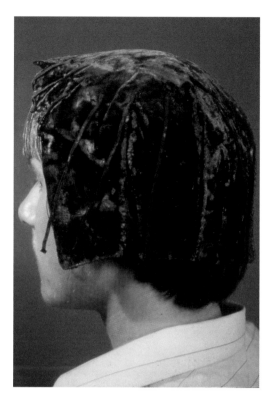

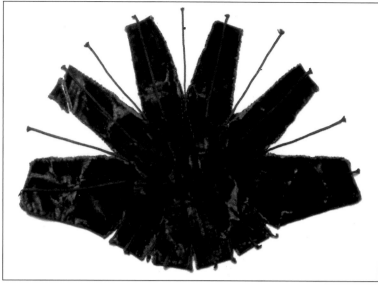

ABOVE A barber-surgeon's cap as recovered from the wreck. This marked his status as a member of the Company of Barber Surgeons. He was a combination of doctor, dentist and pharmacist.

LEFT How the cap was worn.

patients to reduce the amount of blood, are still commemorated in the barber's pole. Robert Symson was surgeon of the *Mary Rose* in 1513, but it is not known who held the office in 1545. A good deal can be told about him, however, from the contents of his chest. His steel cutting tools have naturally been lost, but he possessed several syringes for the painful treatment of gonorrhoea, and bowls that were probably used for bleeding. He had wooden, pewter and pottery containers holding a variety of herbal remedies, including fern oil for

LEFT The barber-surgeon's wooden chest and some of its contents, found almost intact because it was surrounded with compacted clay. Despite this equipment and a supply of herbs and medicines, his techniques were primitive and often highly painful.

melancholy, pine resin for ulcers and wounds, and beeswax mixed with poppy oil to treat the imbalance of body humours. As well as wounds in action or by accident, he had to treat a crew with various existing ailments including bad teeth, rickets, scurvy and badly set fractures.

The carpenter had probably learned his craft by apprenticeship, either at sea or in a shipyard. In the *Mary Rose* he had a cabin/storeroom on the main deck. He had an unknown coterie of assistants – mates or crew – and the number of sea chests found in the *Mary Rose* suggests around six, plus caulkers who would specialise

in filling the spaces between the planks to keep the ship watertight. There may well have been other craftsmen such as coopers on board. The list of 1512 suggests there were 20 'servitours' or servants on board. These could have been apprentices, but it is more likely that they were the personal attendants for the officers. They do not appear as a separate item on later lists, but there can be no doubt that they were carried, perhaps counted among the soldiers.

Seamen

The rest of the crew was divided into three main groups – mariners, soldiers and gunners. In 1511 the Howard brothers fitted out ships to seek out the errant privateer Sir Andrew Barton. According to an Elizabethan ballad King Henry promised:

Then bowmen and gunners shalt thou have
And choose them over my realm so free;
Besides good mariners, and ship-boys,
To guide the great ship on the sea.

In 1512 the *Mary Rose* had 411 men in her complement, not including Howard, Wyndham and two pilots. These were made up of 120 mariners, 251 soldiers, 20 gunners and 20 'servitours' or servants. The number of soldiers was very high, perhaps because some of them were intended to take part in the land operations. In 1522 this had changed radically, with 244 mariners, 126 soldiers and 30 gunners to a total of 403 when adding the

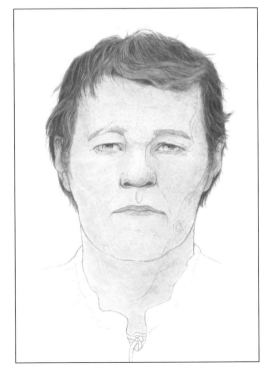

admiral, master and fleet treasurer. According to the Anthony Roll she ended up with a total complement of 415 including 200 seamen, 185 soldiers and 30 gunners. Perhaps the increase in the proportion of soldiers reflects the fact that they were easier to recruit and train, and mariners were in short supply by that time.

In the *Henri Grace à Dieu* or *Great Harry* the master was assisted by a mate and it is likely that the situation was similar in the *Mary Rose*, although she had a crew of 300 mariners rather than the 200 in the Anthony Roll. It is possible that the master and his mate alternated in charge of the sailing of the ship, which was practicable during the relatively short voyages undertaken in those days. The *Great Harry* had four quartermasters who supervised the steering. The much smaller *Elizabeth* of around 120 tons had the same quota in 1513, which suggests the number was constant in different sizes of vessel. The quartermasters had two mates, perhaps one per watch. To the seamen the most prominent figure was the boatswain, holding one of the most ancient titles in the navy. He was in charge of the maintenance of the rigging and boats, he mustered the crew and perhaps allocated their duties. In the *Complaint of Scotland* he was the master's right-hand man, climbing up the mast before the ship set sail to see if any other ships were in sight. He had at least one mate.

Henry's navy did not train its own seamen; indeed, it was 300 years after his death before the Royal Navy ceased to rely on the merchant service for its manpower. They were recruited on the approach of war by compulsion or volunteering. In a sense all merchant seamen had an equal chance of rising to mate or master, for literacy and numeracy were not needed so much in the days when navigational information was mostly carried in the head. But according to William Bourne, many lacked ambition and training:

For I do see a great number that do occupy the sea, that have no sight almost at all in their science, although they have occupied the sea a long time, which is a strange case, that those men that have had the dealing therewith to be utterly void of knowledge, their masters to have both knowledge and cunning, and that they be altogether ignorant, which is occasion that I do think that the expert masters indeed, do seldom instruct their company.

Merchant seamen were still relatively demotic in another way too. In theory they followed the 13th-century Rules of Oleron, in which the ship was run as a kind of cooperative, with the crew often being allocated space to carry cargoes of their own as part of their payment. Before departure the master was expected to ask the crew: 'Gentlemen, what think you of this wind?' He might take a majority decision, and if he sailed against it he would be liable for any damage caused. Corporal punishment was not severe – if the master struck one of the mariners with his fist or open hand he was to tolerate the first stroke, but was entitled to resist any further blows. The laws were mostly about shares in the cargo and the running of merchant ships. They were clearly less relevant in bigger ships and those run on military lines like the *Mary Rose*, but nevertheless a copy of the Rules was ordered to be 'set in the main mast to be read as occasion shall serve'. The mariners tended to value their independence and resist military subjection, which might explain Sir

LEFT The reconstructed face of an officer, identified by the call or whistle found with him. He had apparently done manual work in his youth and risen in rank. *(The Mary Rose Trust/Oscar Nilsson)*

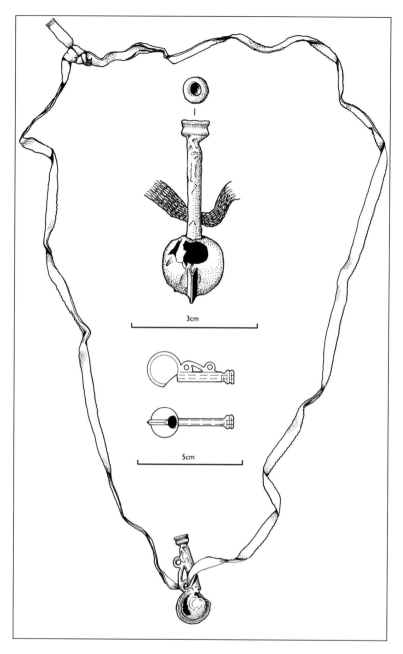

LEFT AND BELOW Silver whistle or call, and the ribbon by which it was hung round the neck as a badge of office. Five were recovered in total, and they were used by petty officers as a means of communicating orders and performing rituals.

3cm

5cm

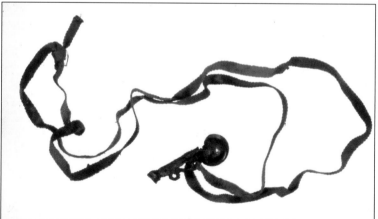

George Carew's final remark in 1545, that he had 'a sort of knaves, whom he could not rule'. According to another account: 'He had in his ship a hundred mariners, the worst of them being able to be master in the best ship within the realm, and these so maligned and disdained one another, that, refusing to do that which they should do, were careless [to do] that which was most needful in necessary. …'

During the First French War Sir Edward Howard was charged with raising the men himself by feudal means, as he undertook to provide 3,000 men, including 1,233 mariners, 'harnessed and arrayed for war'. Although compulsion was probably used to a certain extent, there is no sign of any resistance – the right of a lord to raise men for war was taken for granted, and the king paid reasonably well at 5s per month. Victuals were good and plentiful in theory, even if they were not always delivered in practice. 'Prest' money simply meant an advance in wages, and was not yet connected with the notorious press gangs of later years. Among those involved in recruitment were W. Forde, a lodesman of Bristol who was employed for 40 days, and Myles Smith who gathered together 28 seamen. 'Diverse lords, knights and gentlemen' as well as 'diverse captains and other masters of ships' were paid six pence per man for every twelve miles they travelled to join the fleet.

The feudal system worked best with peasants who were tied to the land rather than highly mobile seamen, and the recruitment process was taken over more and more by the state. By the 1540s there are signs that naval service was less popular, partly because the proportion of mariners on board a warship had increased, and partly because privateering offered greater rewards. Impressment was common by the 1540s, during Henry VIII's war with France. In 1544 it was reported that the king had 'arrested all ships at present in

the harbours of this realm, and is about to put in order more than 150 sail'. Robert Legge of Harwich was paid 40s for himself and two horses, to ride round the ports of Essex 'for presting mariners to Deptford Strond'. Viscount Lisle, the admiral, was given authority 'to take up and provide in all places, as well within franchises and liberties as without, such and as many shipmasters, mariners, shipwrights, soldiers, gunners and other able persons as our said cousin shall think meet for the furniture and manning of the said ships'.

In July 1545 it was reported that the sheriff of Devon had 'laid out certain sums of money for the conduct and prest money of such mariners as be took up to go to Portsmouth'. This was enough to disrupt normal life, and it was reported from Exeter: 'As most of the fishermen here are taken from hence as mariners to serve the King, no fish is to be had, and women are going out fishing, and sometimes are chased by Frenchmen.' Even enemy prisoners could be used on board ship as necessary; according to the instructions to Admiral Woodhouse in 1545, his ships were to 'take all Frenchmen and Scots as good prize, taking the men into their own ships to serve in the same as drudges'. In 1545 the government issued a proclamation that 'no mariner or soldier or other person serving or prest to serve in the Kings ships land from the same without a testimonial signed by their captain'. The same proclamation raised the wages of seamen from 5s to 6s 8d per month, and this seems to have been high enough to allay discontent.

There is no clear definition of the mariner's skills from this period, but it can be conjectured that he was adept at many kinds of knots and ropework, that he could climb the rigging when needed, haul on ropes and push at capstan bars, row and steer the ship's boats and perhaps the ship herself, as well as helping with guns when needed and fighting hand-to-hand.

The gunners

Some years later William Bourne wrote that 'we English men have not been counted but of late days to become good gunners' and 'for the knowledge of it, other nations and countries have tasted better thereof … for that English men have had but little instructions but that they have learned of the Dutchmen or Flemings in the time of King Henry the Eighth'. Certainly Henry's gunfounders included the Arcana family from Italy and the Frenchman Peter Baude, as well as the Owens of England or Wales, and they may have brought gunners with them or trained them. But English gunners were not uncommon and the Elizabethan ballad mentions Peter Simon, 'the ablest gunner in all the realm', although he was 70 years old.

It is not clear how far the sea gunner was separated from the land gunner, and undoubtedly they had some shared knowledge. According to Bourne, a gunner had to recognise the quality of his powder, which might vary considerably and affect accuracy. He should know whether each gun under his care was truly bored, the windage or gap between the shot and the barrel, the shape of each individual shot, the use of wads to pack the powder tightly or loosely and the position or 'standing' of his piece. He had to know its length and its 'dispart' – the difference between the diameter at the breech and muzzle – to aid his aiming. The sea gunner probably made little use of the gunner's quadrant, which helped the land gunner, for accurate aim over any distance was almost impossible with a moving ship. The sea gunner had to ensure that his pieces were 'fast breeched' so that they did not break free and become the proverbial loose cannons. He needed to take especial care of his powder, exposed neither to fire nor damp. The inside of

each gun had to be kept dry and the touch hole clear, and it was recommended that a master gunner should keep a record of the dispart of every piece 'and mark it upon the piece, or else in some book or tale, and name every piece what it is, and where it doth lie in the ship'. But Bourne had to agree that the English made better sea gunners, 'for that they are hardy or without fear about their ordnance' and that 'they are handsome about their ordnance in ships, on the sea, & c.'.

The *Mary Rose* carried 20 or 30 gunners for most of her recorded career. It is difficult to explain why this number rose and fell, and it is suspiciously round to be fully accurate. It was never enough to provide a gunner for each weapon – the ship had 20 gunners in 1512 and 78 guns of all sizes in 1514. By 1545 she had 30 gunners for 91 guns. Possibly one gunner was attached to each of the large guns (with only those on one side being used at any given moment), while others each supervised a group of smaller guns. Already the senior member of the branch was becoming known as *the* gunner – a post held by Andrew Fische in 1513.

Soldiers

The written records tell us even less about the soldiers on board the *Mary Rose* than the sailors, except for the numbers carried. There were 411 in the summer of 1512, but most of these were probably part of the invasion force for Gascony and were not intended to serve permanently on the ship. In 1522 the number dropped as low as 126, but in 1524 and 1545–46 it was 185. English

soldiers were recruited in two different ways, either as part of the retinue of a feudal lord or in a more modern system, although the militia organised on a county basis. It is likely that the men of the *Mary Rose* were recruited by feudal means – the militia was only intended for home defence, while men on board ship might be sent anywhere. There were no 'regular' soldiers in modern terms, except perhaps in the regard that the aristocracy was educated and trained to lead in battle and, in addition, large numbers of foreign mercenaries were taken on.

Land forces were developing an organisation by companies of around 100 men, so there might have been two slightly smaller companies on the *Mary Rose*. Each would be headed by a captain, with a 'petty captain' as second in command. A company normally had four or five 'vintenars' each in charge of 20–25 men. A few decades later they would be known as corporals. The term 'sergeant' was changing in meaning, from a servant or common soldier to the corporal's superior, but it was probably not used in that sense in the early days of the *Mary Rose*'s life. There was no real concept of uniform, but one of the 46 leather tunics recovered from the ship had crosses sewn on to it – perhaps a relic of an earlier campaign, or a sign of the devotion of the wearer. They are often shown in contemporary illustrations, for example the Siege of Boulogne.

The soldiers could shoot longbows and some may have been professional archers. The English army was often criticised for retaining this obsolete weapon in the days of gunpowder, but it had advantages of reliability in wet conditions, and some learned to use it with great pride – the longbow was a weapon close to the English heart, with the legend of Robin Hood and the great victory at Agincourt. It was also a populist weapon in that a peasant farmer or city tradesman could stop or at least dismount an armoured knight. Around this time the citizens of London complained of ditches and hedges in the fields round the city, so that they could not practise. They responded by direct action one morning, when 'within a short space all the hedges about the city were cast down, and ditches filled up'. Later in the century there were still more than 160 aiming marks in Finsbury Fields, with names such as Pinder,

ABOVE Soldiers from the same picture, assembled in a tighter formation on open ground, with groups of archers and officers standing close by.

BELOW Groups of archers can be seen practising in Finsbury Fields just north of London, from a map of *c*1540. This was one of the main functions of the open space around the city, and archers were very proud of their skills.

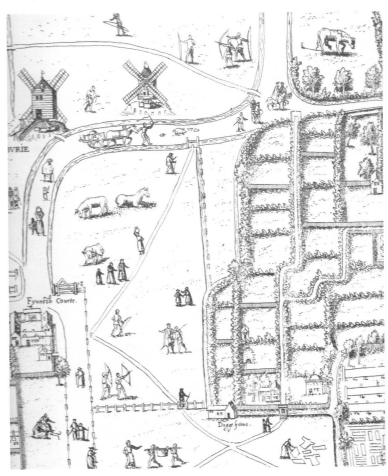

Lurching Lake, Queen's Stake and Hearty Goodwill. Hugh Latimer, born near Leicester around 1485, describes his boyhood:

My poor father was diligent to teach me to shoot, as to learn any other thing, and so I think other men did their children. He taught me how to draw, how to lay my body in my bow, and not to draw with strength of arms as other nations do, but with strength of body. I had my bows brought to me according to my age and strength; as I increased in them, so my bows were made bigger; for men never shoot well except they be brought up to it.

A high proportion of skeletons recovered from the wreck of the *Mary Rose* – up to 19% by one count – revealed a condition known as 'os acromiale' in which the small acromion bone failed to unite with the scapula on maturity. This was possibly a result of early and continued training with the longbow, and most of these men may have been professional archers, perhaps part of the personal retinue of Sir George Carew – although the same condition might have been caused by hauling on ropes and so on. According to the Anthony Roll the ship was allocated 250 yew longbows and 400 sheaves of 24 arrows each, while other men may well have brought their own weapons. Some 172 longbows, 2,302 complete arrows and 7,834 fragments have been recovered from the wreck.

BELOW Scapulae from a skeleton recovered from the hold. The separation of the acromion (indicated by arrows) and other features, suggest that the man may have been an archer. The same condition has been found on many of the skeletons from the wreck.

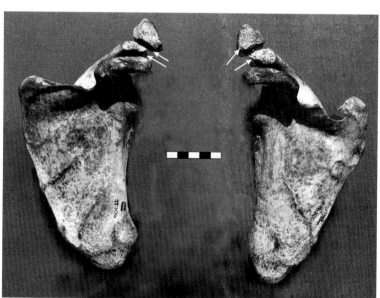

Other soldiers used the arquebus, a firearm activated by a matchlock. Skill with a gun was accepted as an alternative to archery in the statutes of the time and it was easier to acquire, even if the weapon was more expensive, heavier and slow to reload. The surviving portion of a Tudor map of London shows a pair of arquebusiers practising in Finsbury Fields alongside at least 17 men with bows. Archers and arquebusiers also carried hand weapons such as swords and daggers, which could be used in boarding, and might be ready with pike and bill to defend the ship.

Duties

Large warships had grown beyond the stage when men could be allocated duties casually and individually, and much organisation was needed. There exists a station list of the *Great Harry,* perhaps for setting the sails. It gives a total of 514 men, which is less than the full complement of 700 but far more than the seaman complement of 301 in 1545. This suggests that soldiers were used to do heavy, unskilled work such as pushing at the capstan and hauling on ropes. Deducting the 50 gunners (who would regard themselves above menial work and would not have the skills of the seamen) and a certain numbers of officers and gentlemen and their servants, the figure of 514 seamen and soldiers for manual work seems entirely credible. Applying this to the 200 mariners, 185 soldiers and 30 gunners of the *Mary Rose* on her last voyage, it might be expected that around 320 men were needed for manual labour when setting sail.

The station list begins with what might be considered special duties for skilled seamen. Some 70 men were allocated to the boats of the *Great Harry,* for they probably had to stand by to help with the anchor if needed. Scaling this down for the *Mary Rose,* there might be approximately 24 allocated to the 'great boat', 12 to the 'cock' from which the coxswain took his title, and 6 to the 'gellywatte' or jollyboat, a total of 42. More skilled men were needed up the rigging, perhaps two dozen in the case of the *Mary Rose,* including 8 in the main top, 4 each in the fore top and main mizzen top, and 2 each in the bonaventure top, the 'little top upon the main

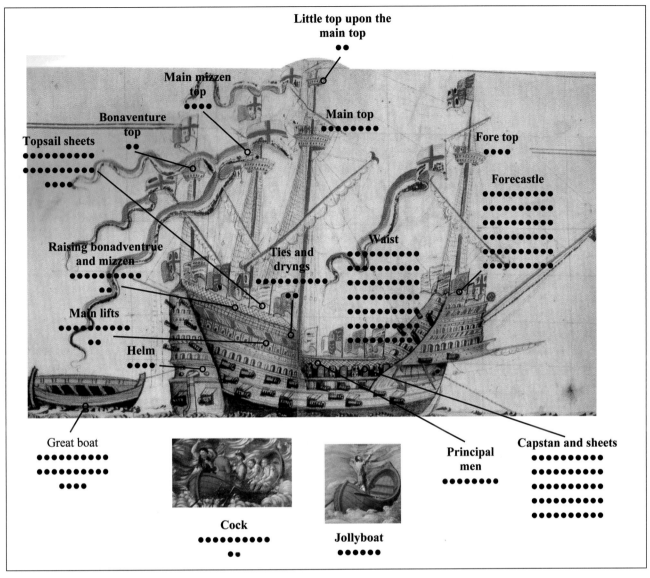

Little top upon the
main top
● ●

Main mizzen
top
● ● ● ●

Bonaventure
top
● ●

Topsail sheets
● ● ● ● ● ● ● ● ● ●
● ● ● ● ● ● ● ● ● ●
● ● ● ●

Main top
● ● ● ● ● ● ● ● ●

Fore top
● ● ● ●

Forecastle
● ● ● ● ● ● ● ● ● ●
● ● ● ● ● ● ● ● ● ●
● ● ● ● ● ● ● ● ● ●
● ● ● ● ● ● ● ● ● ●
● ● ● ● ● ● ● ● ● ●
● ● ● ● ● ● ● ● ● ●

Raising bonadventrue
and mizzen
● ● ● ● ● ● ● ● ●
● ●

Ties and
dryngs
● ● ● ● ● ● ● ● ●
● ●

Waist
● ● ● ● ● ● ● ● ●
● ● ● ● ● ● ● ● ●
● ● ● ● ● ● ● ● ●
● ● ● ● ● ● ● ● ●
● ● ● ● ● ● ● ● ●

Main lifts
● ● ● ● ● ● ● ●
● ●

Helm
● ● ● ●

Great boat
● ● ● ● ● ● ● ● ● ●
● ● ● ● ● ● ● ● ● ●
● ● ● ●

Cock
● ● ● ● ● ● ● ● ● ●
● ●

Jollyboat
● ● ● ● ● ●

Principal
men
● ● ● ● ● ● ● ●

Capstan and sheets
● ● ● ● ● ● ● ● ● ●
● ● ● ● ● ● ● ● ● ●
● ● ● ● ● ● ● ● ● ●
● ● ● ● ● ● ● ● ● ●
● ● ● ● ● ● ● ● ● ●

top', the 'little top upon the fore top' and the 'little top upon the main mizzen top'.

The forecastle needed perhaps 60 men. Others, presumably soldiers and less skilled or fit seamen, were allocated to duties about the decks. There would be around 70 in the waist in the centre of the main deck, chiefly to haul on ropes. The main capstan and the main sheets employed 50 men, with perhaps a dozen on the second deck in the forecastle for the main lifts to level the yards, and the same number on the third deck for ties and 'dryngs', which would also be used to raise and position the mainsail. There were about two dozen men on the third deck for the topsail sheets, and half that number to raise the bonaventure and main mizzen sails. To supervise the operation,

8 'principal men' were stationed on the 'strikes' or ropes of the mainsail; 4 sailors were to man the helm of the *Henri Grace à Dieu*, and it is likely that the *Mary Rose* needed the same number, presumably the 4 quartermasters. Thus a total of 318 men would be ready to carry out manual work when the *Mary Rose* set sail.

Life on board

There was no central victualling organisation during Henry's reign, and food was supplied by local contractors or officials sent from London. There was plenty of scope for fraud, and in April 1513 Howard complained that meat supposed to supply the men for two months would not last more than five weeks,

ABOVE Suggested distribution of the crew of the *Mary Rose*, perhaps for setting sail, with the base picture from the Anthony Roll. The large numbers of men in the waist were probably for hauling on ropes and pushing at the capstan, while the men of the forecastle were likely there to help stow the anchors. Each dot represents a man.

as there was too high a proportion of salt in the barrels, 'and when the pieces keepeth the number, when they should be penny pieces they be scant halfpenny pieces, and where two pieces should make a mess, three will do but serve'. He wrote that 'never was an army so falsely victualled'.

Two casks of beef were found on the orlop deck, and it could be boiled in the two kettles in the galley. Pork was usually split and hung and fish was mostly found in baskets. In theory each member of the crew was entitled to a gallon of beer a day, which provided a large proportion of his calorie intake. He had 1lb of ship's biscuit, which accounted for most of the rest of the calorific value, along with 1lb of pork on Sunday and Thursday, 2lb of beef on Monday and Tuesday, with fish, when available, on the 'meatless' days of Wednesday, Friday and Saturday. He had peas with the pork and 2oz of butter on each of the fish days, along with 4oz of cheese. The term 'mess' was used, for example by Edward Howard on 5 April 1513, but probably in the sense of a prepared dish. It is not clear if a group of men got together to form 'messes', as in later years. That concept depends on the existence of a table or mess, derived from the Spanish, but none of these

ABOVE The ship's bell, used to mark the time. One stroke was rung for each half hour after the watch changed, and the watch ended with eight bells, for the cycle to start again. The bell could also be used to summon the crew.

RIGHT A selection of bowls, tankards and other tableware recovered from the wreck. Wooden items were in daily use by the crew as they were cheap and almost unbreakable.

ABOVE A selection of objects that might have been found on the captain's table. All except the foodstuffs, tablecloth and candle were recovered from the wreck.

LEFT Pewter tankards, bowls and a selection of pewter objects including bowls and a syringe, mainly belonging to the surgeon and other officers.

ABOVE Bowls of various sizes. Sixty of them were found in the ship, made from beech or alder and occasionally from birch, elm or oak. Most have a flat base to allow them to stand on a table or on the deck.

ABOVE A wooden tankard reconstructed from recovered parts. It is made in barrel-fashion with staves held together by wooden hoops, with a wooden lid to protect the contents, probably beer.

RIGHT One of many marks found on bowls, probably used to indicate ownership in a largely illiterate society.

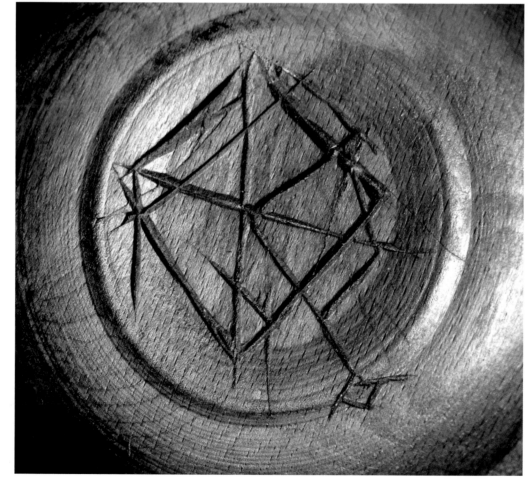

have been found except for those that were obviously intended for the officers. Pewter cutlery was probably used by the officers; the men had wooden bowls, plates and spoons, with tankards made of staves in the same manner as casks. Drinking bowls and tankards were often very personal items, carved with the owner's name or symbol.

A shortage of victuals often had a decisive effect on campaigns. When the English fleet was made ready in March 1513 it was well equipped with men and guns, but Howard begged: 'For God's sake, haste your Council to send us down our victual.' When off the Breton coast, 'for of ten days ... there was no man in all the army that had but one meal a day and one drink'. Stores arrived, but not enough. It was not just a lust for feudal glory that caused Howard to launch his premature and fatal attack on the French galleys in April 1513. There was only three days' food on board the ships, and he felt the need to act

ABOVE Parts of a leather jerkin found in the wreck, a common garment especially with soldiers and archers. This is a comparatively simple one, front fastening with no decoration.

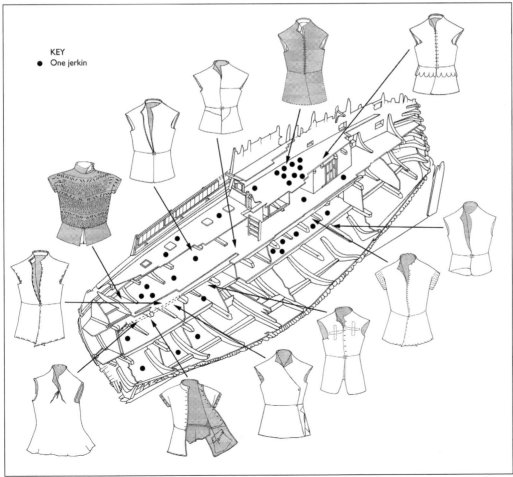

KEY
● One jerkin

LEFT Some of the 46 jerkins recovered, and the sites where they were found. Most fasten at the centre, others at the side and a few have a crossover front, such as the one third from the left on the bottom.

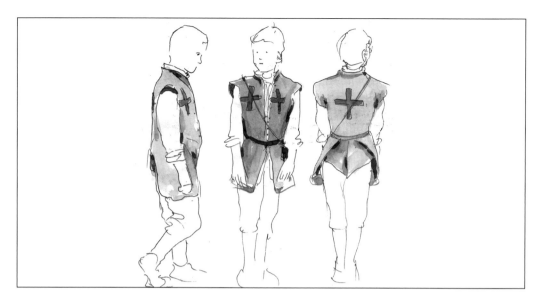

RIGHT Reconstruction of a jerkin with crosses sewn on. The original is the only one to be decorated in this way, although the crosses themselves have not survived and are only indicated by stitch holes.

RIGHT One of many shoes found in the ship. Most of them are welted, with the lower part made up of an insole, welt, mid-sole edging and outer sole, a form of construction still used today.

quickly. And when his brother took command of the fleet in Plymouth Sound, 'they had a great default of victual and had not in their board for three days'. From 1513 it was decreed that ships intended for winter service should be supplied with food for two months, although that remained an aspiration. In 1522 the Earl of Surrey complained that some of his ships only had supplies for eight days.

Scant knowledge exists about the daily life of the crew. It can be presumed that all of them were on duty during short voyages, intricate manoeuvres such as raising the anchor or

RIGHT A backgammon or tabula board found in the carpenter's cabin along with eight counters. It is made of oak inlaid with yew and spruce or larch. Sailors also played with dice and eleven were recovered in different locations.

tacking, and in battle. Otherwise the seamen at least were divided into two watches – an ambiguous term that might mean a four-hour period of duty, or the team of men allocated to it. Little is known about how the men slept when off watch. The hammock was not discovered until the end of the century, but a very small amount of hay has been found, mainly on the orlop deck where mattresses could have been stowed during action. Since the area under the forecastle was reserved for officers and the orlop was crowded with stores, it must be assumed that they slept on the main deck, even though it was interrupted by rising knees and gun carriages. Life cannot have been comfortable at sea.

LEFT A leather flask that probably belonged to an officer. It was found in a personal chest which also contained a coin balance, two shoes, an ankle boot and two combs. It is decorated with two vine scrolls and a shield on each side of the centre.

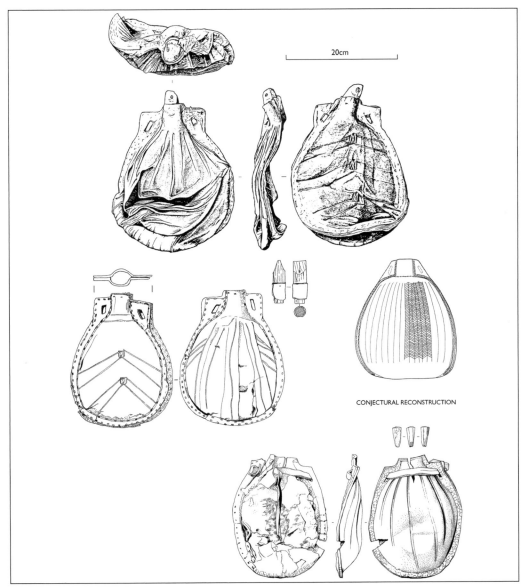

20cm

CONJECTURAL RECONSTRUCTION

LEFT A selection of leather drinking flasks as used by officers and crew. Some are highly decorated, others are plain. They would have contained liquid, possibly wine.

Chapter Four

Sailing the Mary Rose

The *Mary Rose* was one of the best sailing ships of her day, even if she would have seemed sluggish in later centuries. She relied heavily on favourable winds and the use of tides and it required special skills to sail the ship and to navigate with little in the way of charts.

OPPOSITE The *Mary Rose* in her prime, c.1545. Scholars will continue to debate the number of decks there were at the bow or stern. This depiction shows two decks at the stern, while some others show three. (© *W.H.Bishop*)

The *Mary Rose* was totally dependent on sails for her movement. The galleys she fought alongside and against had far narrower hulls and lighter construction. A sailing ship on the other hand needed a broad hull to prevent too much heeling in the wind, so oars were impracticable and there is no sign that they were ever fitted to the *Mary Rose*. The only realistic alternative to sailing was 'warping' – laying an anchor out ahead and hauling the ship up to it with the capstan, or attaching a rope to a fixed point and hauling the ship forward.

Sailing qualities

There is no doubt that the *Mary Rose* sailed well by the standards of the time. In 1513 Howard wrote to Henry that she was, 'the flower, I trow, of all ships that ever sailed'. She was equally good in the Second French War. In June 1522 Vice-Admiral Sir William Fitzwilliam wrote to the king that there would be 'a hard choice' between the *Mary Rose* and the new great ship *Henri Grace à Dieu* or *Great Harry* with the wind behind, and implied that *Mary Rose* was the more weatherly when going into the wind. These two sailed better than any others, except a galley, which might well surge ahead if able to 'veer the sheet' as she would do with the wind behind, but she had little underwater to prevent her being blown sideways and would make little progress in a less than perfect wind.

Why did the *Mary Rose* sail so well? With no precise data on any other ship of the time, it is impossible to be sure. Perhaps her hull was well formed, to quite an advanced design. The use of several sweeps in midships may have helped to create a shape with the centres of gravity and flotation at suitable levels. It is significant that the *Great Harry*, another new ship, also sailed well, suggesting that both were built using the most modern design methods. But there were other factors in good sailing. New ships probably had clean bottoms, relatively free of weeds and barnacles, which reduced friction. And they most likely had the pick of officers and crew, who would know how to get the best out of a ship.

The winds

No one was more dependent on the weather than the seaman of the days of sail. If there was no wind or it came from the wrong sector he might wait for weeks before leaving harbour. If there was too much wind, there was a risk of foundering if he put to sea.

RIGHT The *Henri Grace à Dieu* or *Great Harry* as drawn by Anthony Anthony. The ship was launched in 1514 and was larger than the *Mary Rose.* She is shown here with taller masts and more sails and guns. *(Pepys Library, Magdalene College, Cambridge)*

LEFT Plymouth Sound, *c*1539. The Sound itself was too open for ships to anchor there for any length of time, but they could find shelter in the Cattewater or behind St Nicholas's Island. *(British Library, Cotton MS, Augustus I i 35)*

The *Mary Rose* saw nothing of the circular wind pattern of the North Atlantic, or the local and seasonal winds of the Mediterranean. Instead, she had to cope with the travelling depressions that moved across the British Isles from the Atlantic, except when they were blocked by high pressure. Her sailors knew nothing of that terminology, but they were fully aware that the weather was largely unpredictable. British winds did not have names like those of the Mediterranean or the oceans and might come from any direction. That was an advantage in that no parts of the coast were completely inaccessible given time, but commanders often had to deal with the impatience of the king. Trapped in Plymouth in 1513, Thomas, Lord Howard, wrote to Cardinal Wolsey 'desiring you to beseech the King's grace not to think no laxness in me for our long abode here … for I assure you the fault is in the wind and not in me, as I am sure every skilled man can show you'.

In that instance the newly appointed Lord Howard had anchored his ships in three sections in Plymouth Sound. Some of them, including the storeships and the *Peter Pomegranate* were in the Cattewater to the east of the Sound. Most of the large ships, probably including the *Mary Rose*, were anchored behind St Nicholas's Island, while others, presumably in the Sound itself, were 'moored together in strait room' where they were 'in great danger' and did 'nightly fall together' or collide with one another. There was no single wind, except from the north, which would allow all the ships to leave at once, and westerlies prevailed for nine days.

In 1539 50 ships (not including the *Mary Rose*) waited at Calais for two weeks for a favourable wind to carry Henry's future bride, Anne of Cleves, across the 30 miles to Deal in Kent – but the king was shatteringly disappointed when he finally caught sight of the 'Flanders mare'. Even in the best conditions,

high speed was not expected of a ship. In 1527 Cardinal Wolsey joined a ship at Dover between three and four in the morning. When he was in Calais by nine, he considered it a 'good and pleasant passage', at a speed of perhaps five knots, if the ship had sailed at four.

Educated men were aware of theories of weather originating with the ancient Greeks and Romans. These did not take account of very different climatic conditions between British waters and the Mediterranean. It is not clear if any of the *Mary Rose*'s admirals or captains had the education or inclination to follow such ideas, but masters and seamen were more practical men and tended to use experience rather than theory. William Bourne prided himself on his plain writing and knew a large number of seafarers from his home town on the River Thames. He was aware that if the wind was following the movement of the sun, for example proceeding from east to south, then fair weather would follow – in modern terms an area of high pressure was on its way. If the wind was altering in the other direction, for instance south then west, a depression was approaching, bringing rain and possibly strong winds. Other signs included the cloud formation: 'If that the sky aloft be full of long streams like unto horses and mares tails, that is a token of great southerly winds to follow'; and indeed wispy cirrus clouds could herald the advance of a depression. A red sky in the evening was a sign of good weather, while in the morning it meant that the area of high pressure was moving away to the east and a depression was likely to develop. And there were many who believed that an increase in pain suffered from such as arthritis and sciatica signified bad weather.

Tides

Tides were more predictable than winds and were particularly strong in British waters. The *Mary Rose* did not venture into the second and third highest tidal ranges in the world – St Michael's Bay in France and the Bristol Channel – but she spent most of her time in the Portsmouth area where the water might rise and fall by up to 15ft. She had to encounter or avoid terrifying tide races such as the one off Portland, which might reach a speed of six knots, as fast as any ship could go in normal circumstances.

ABOVE The harbour of Calais from a chart of around 1540. As an English possession until 1558, it served as a base on the continent and was recorded several times in drawings like this, often showing ships in various positions. *(British Library, Cotton MS, Augustus I Ii f. 70)*

RIGHT A chart showing the tidal movements around England, by Guillaume Brouscon, *c*1540. It was well known that they were controlled by the moon and to a lesser extent the sun. *(British Library, Add. MS, 22721 f. 10v)*

RIGHT Dividers and a wooden disc featuring a compass rose showing all 32 points, deeply incised so that it could be used in the dark, although it is not marked with any precision and could not be used for navigation as such. Possibly it was used for tidal calculations.

Every mariner knew that tides were caused by the moon. Among the skills of Chaucer's shipman in 1387 were,

to reckon well the tides,
The storms and dangers all besides.
His harbour and his moon, his pilotage.

The moon pulled a great body of water up and down the English Channel and the North Sea, but the movement was not instantaneous, and high tide at a particular place might be some hours before or after the moon passed over. Mariners calculated high tide by the position of the moon. Garcie wrote: 'At the Needles of the Isle of Wight without [ie on the seaward side], the moon at the south-east and a point south, full sea [ie high tide]; at the coast of the said isle at a high spring the moon at the south-west, full sea.'

There were two high and two low tides each day. It was well known that high tide one day was a little less than an hour later the next day. William Bourne wrote that 'the course of the tides is nothing else, but to put for every day of the age of the moon one hour, pulling back the fifth part of an hour, being 12 minutes'; that is, 48 minutes later. Tide levels also varied from day to day in a fortnightly cycle, because the pull of the sun also played its part.

Tides had two main effects: the rise and fall, and the currents they created. A falling tide could make it very dangerous to cross a sandbar, as a ship that went aground might

BELOW Using the tide to progress when there was no wind in June 1522. It is not clear whether the ship went north or south of the Isle of Wight; however, the latter appears more possible and seems plausible from what is known about the tides.
(John Lawson)

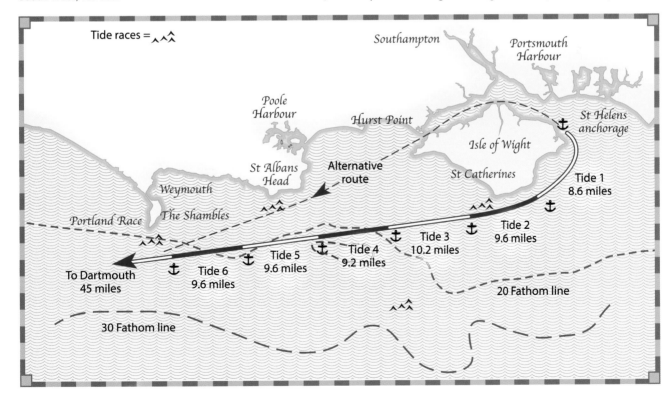

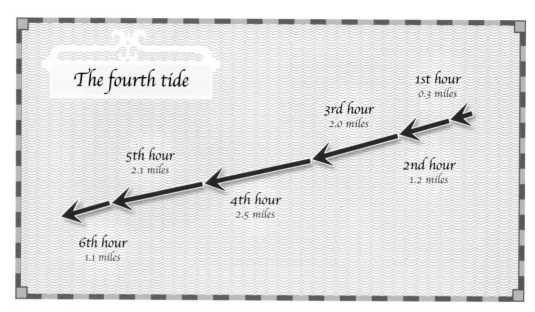

RIGHT The hourly
movement during the
fourth tide from the
diagram overleaf on
page 83. The ship is
likely to move much
faster in the third to
fifth hour when the
current is stronger,
and especially in the
fourth hour.
(John Lawson)

The fourth tide

1st hour
0.3 miles

3rd hour
2.0 miles

2nd hour
1.2 miles

5th hour
2.1 miles

4th hour
2.5 miles

6th hour
1.1 miles

be trapped until the water rose again. The lack of water could also delay the movement of ships. Part of the problem with Anne of Cleves's sojourn at Calais was to find a suitable tide to let the ship leave the shallow harbour, but also to arrive in England before dark. However, the rise and fall of the tide made it easier to clean the bottom of a ship by grounding it deliberately and waiting for the tide to go out. The movement of the tide made navigation difficult if the ship was being pushed sideways, for example in crossing the English Channel. But unlike the wind it was predictable and reliable, and could be used to move ships, as in June 1522 (see diagram overleaf on page 83).

The sails

In 1514 the *Mary Rose* was equipped with six square sails, which were not literally square. The three lower sails, the main and fore courses and the spritsail under the bowsprit, were parallel sided, but the upper ones, the topsails and topgallants, tapered considerably. All of them had a curve, known as the gore, in the lower edge. There were four 'bonnets' or extensions, two each for the fore- and mainsails, intended to be used together and fitted one under the other if necessary. In addition, the ship had three triangular or 'lateen' sails, the mizzen and bonaventure courses and the mizzen topsail. No spare sails were carried except that there were two bonaventures, which may be a clerical error in the record. Part

of a sail was found on the orlop deck of the wreck, but in general there was no possibility of changing sails of different thicknesses to suit the weather.

Sailcloth was woven from hemp and possibly nettle fibre in strips 2ft (0.6m) wide, sewn together to make a sail. A 'bolt rope' was sewn round the edge to strengthen it, with loops known as cringles to attach ropes such as sheets and bowlines. Each sail was cut with a considerable amount of 'bag' in the middle; that is, it was curved in both the horizontal and vertical planes. This might have helped in filling the sail with the wind behind (like a modern spinnaker), but it made it less suitable for sailing close to the wind, when a slightly curved 'aerofoil section' was best. Each sail was attached to its yard by ropes fitted to cringles at each end, and hauled as tight as possible. The central parts of the sail were held to the yard by lighter ropes known as robbands or rope-bands.

Controlling the sails

There were two essential tasks in controlling each sail so that it performed best in the wind at that moment: to set the right amount of sail, and to have it at the correct angle to the wind. Each sail was set by sending men or boys out along its yard to loosen the 'gaskets' or ropes that furled it. Men below hauled on the ropes, known as sheets, attached to the lower corners of the sail. With the courses these led directly to the hull, with the topsails and topgallants they passed through a pulley at the end of the yard below. There was no means of reducing the area of a sail by reefing, as was done in later centuries, but the fore and main courses could be extended by means of the bonnets laced to their lower edges. Otherwise, the master could only control the amount of sail carried by setting or furling the individual sails to suit the conditions. Too much sail in windy conditions would cause the ship to heel over so that the sails would be less efficient, and at worst they might bring her close to capsize. The master also had to consider whether square sails were more appropriate with the wind behind, or lateen sails with it coming over one side of the ship or the other. The balance of the rig was very important; the right sails set towards the bow and stern could be very helpful in steering.

With the wind behind, the yards and sails would be arranged 'square' to the line of motion to catch the maximum amount of wind. On any other point of sailing it was necessary to angle the sail correctly. The yards were managed by means of braces, which led aft towards the deck. A team of men would release the brace on one side of the ship while a larger team hauled on the brace on the other side. The sheets of the upper sails needed no major alteration during this, but those of the courses had to be hauled in and let out in the same way as the braces. The master and his assistants made certain that the sails were at the best angle, with the wind coming over both sides of each, with no flapping.

When sailing close to the wind, it was important to ensure that the sail was not taken aback with the breeze coming on the wrong side. This could be difficult in variable winds, but ropes known as bowlines were attached to the outer edges of each sail to haul it as far forward as possible. Often they were divided into several ropes known as 'crow's feet' at the end nearest to the sail, in order to control as much of the edge as possible.

The mizzen and spritsails

The mizzen was a versatile sail that could be used in several ways. Its primary function was to help the ship sail closer to the wind, as in its usual position between the shrouds it could be set to point closer into the wind than the

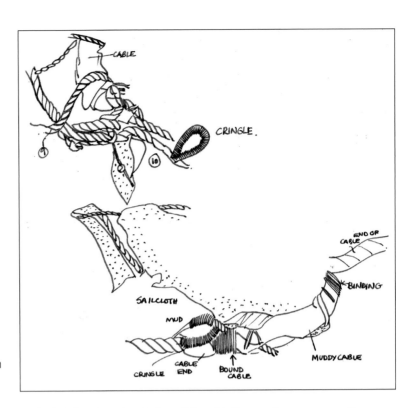

ABOVE A drawing of part of a sail found in the wreck, a very rare glimpse of the motive power of the ship. As well as fragments of sailcloth (probably made from hemp and nettle), there is a cringle for connecting a line.

BELOW The principal ropes attached to the yards and sails of a typical mainmast of the time. The braces and sheets control the angle of the sail to the wind. The bonnet was removed in strong winds.

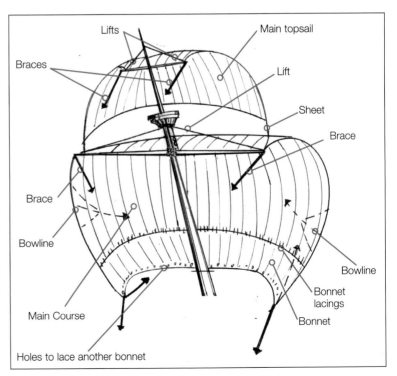

square sails of the mainmast and foremast. But in many of the drawings and paintings of the period the mizzen is to be seen set outside the shrouds. An extreme example is shown in one of the ships off Dartmouth in 1539–40. The mizzen yard is almost parallel to the main yard, and in effect the sail is acting as a square sail. It would not be difficult to set the mizzen yard outside the shrouds, but a good deal of labour would be needed to raise it to the vertical and lift it round, as was often done with Arabian craft. Another situation is shown in one of the ships in the Calais drawing of around 1540. The horizontal edge of the sail, the leech, would normally by set away from the wind, but in this case it is shown pointing into the wind, rather like the edge of a square sail. The bonaventure behind the mizzen carried only a very small sail, but its position gave it a good deal of leverage during manoeuvres.

The spritsail under the bowsprit is not often seen set in pictures of the period, although a ship off Dartmouth in 1539–40 has it in rather a strange configuration. The 1540 map of Calais shows four ships with spritsails set and well filled by wind, while the 1538 drawing of Dover shows several small ships with their sheets hauled well in so that the sails are almost parallel to the bowsprit.

RIGHT **One of the anchors recovered from the** *Mary Rose.* **The stock, an essential part of it, would have been made of wood and is missing, but the arms, spade-like flukes, the long straight shank and the ring can be seen.**

Raising the anchor

Ships like the *Mary Rose* rarely came alongside a pier or jetty except for maintenance or to be laid up. The great majority of voyages started with the raising of the anchor. According to the 1514 list she carried a sheet anchor, to be used in emergencies, two bower anchors that were kept hung from the bows when not in use, two 'destrells' whose definition is unknown and a 'cagger' or kedge, which would be rowed out in front of the ship when warping. Parts of three anchors were found in the bow and one on the upper deck at the end of the waist.

Each anchor had a wooden stock (just over 3m long in the case of the most intact of the *Mary Rose* examples). This would lie horizontally on the sea bottom when the anchor was in use. At the other end of an iron shank (3.15m long) were two arms with a total span of about 2m. One of these would bury itself in the seabed and its spade-like fluke would prevent it being dragged along. The anchor cable, a thick rope made in nine strands and 15in in circumference, was attached to a ring on the other end of the shank.

The cable was hauled up using a capstan, which is listed in the ship's inventory but has not been found. Around 50 men might be employed in pushing at its bars. If a ship was held by two anchors to prevent her swinging with the tide, she was hauled up to one while the cable of the other one was let out or 'veered'. When that was raised, the cable of the second anchor was pulled in. As it broke surface, a party of skilled men

RIGHT **Details of an anchor and stocks found on the upper deck at the end of the waist. The upper stock was made in two pieces. The lower one was discovered with its anchor in the bow area.**

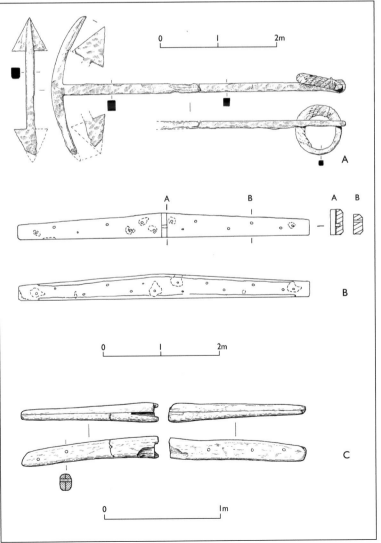

RIGHT The principle of anchoring, from Falconer's *Marine Dictionary* of 1769. The stock rests on the bottom to make sure that the arm and flukes on one side bury themselves. The pull has to be reasonably horizontal so a suitable length of cable is needed. In this case a buoy is being used to mark the position of the anchor.

RIGHT Ships at anchor off Calais. Their cables seem to be taut so they may be in a strong wind or current, which would ensure that they are all facing in the same direction, although it might put the ships at risk of dragging.
(British Library)

RIGHT AND FAR RIGHT A possible 'cat-hook' recovered from the bow castle area between 2003 and 2005. This could have been used to hook up one end of the anchor shank so that it could be lashed against the side to prevent danger to the hull.

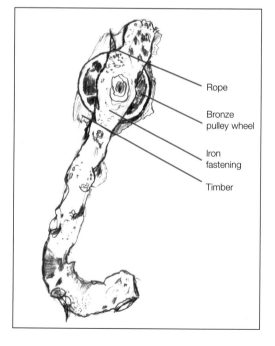

Rope

Bronze pulley wheel

Iron fastening

Timber

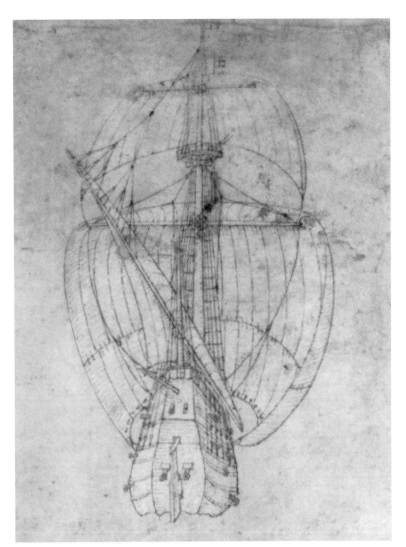

stood by to engage the ring of the anchor with
the 'cat tackle' and heave it up to the forecastle.
Then they would hook the other end of the shank
with the 'fish tackle' and tug it level, securing it as
tightly as possible to prevent it swinging about. In
the meantime, men loosed the sails while others
hauled on the sheets to set them.

Points of sailing

Given a certain amount of wind, large ships
of the time often sailed with the wind almost
right behind. In March 1513 Sir Edward Howard
wrote that a wind from the west-south-west
was 'very good for us' when progressing almost
due eastward out of the Thames Estuary, so it
was only about 20° away from directly astern.
Similarly, in May that year his brother considered
a wind from the west-south-west, immediately
astern, would be perfect for sailing up the Channel
towards Southampton – provided he could get
out of Plymouth Sound. This was different from
what modern seafarers expect; they have found
that a sail is more efficient if the wind is coming
over one side or the other of the ship, and the
sail is operating, in a sense, like an aeroplane
wing set vertically rather than a parachute. In
1522 Howard, now Earl of Surrey, considered
a northerly wind to be 'meetly good' or just
adequate, to sail mainly west by south towards
Dartmouth; that is, it was just aft of the beam.

Ships generally sailed best with the wind
coming over the side, so that all the sails could
be filled and the aerofoil section of the sails was
at its most effective. If the wind was forward of
that then the ship was said to be close-hauled

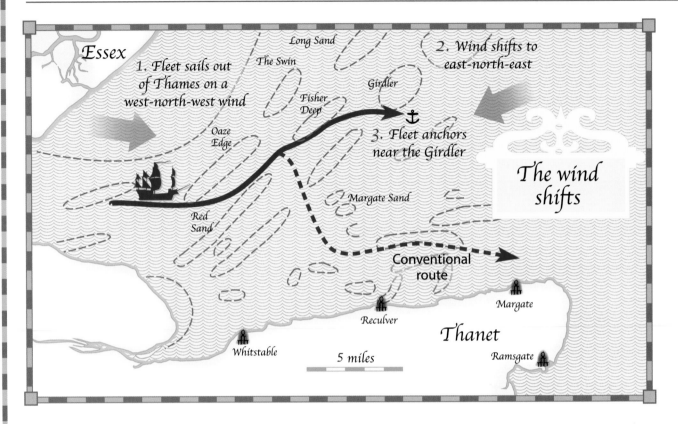

The *Mary Rose* proved her sailing qualities in March 1513 during a voyage out of the Thames Estuary towards the anchorage in The Downs off the Kent coast. She did well on all points of sailing – with the wind behind **[1]**, with it coming over the beam when she caught up with other ships **[6]**, and when tacking or making 'many turns' to sail into the wind **[11]**.

The wind shifts

[1] Coming eastwards out of the Thames in March 1513, Sir Edward Howard's fleet started with a favourable west-north-west wind, which **[2]** veered through 140 degrees to the east-north-east, preventing any progress. **[3]** The ships anchored near the Girdler Sand north-west of Margate, though some of the smaller ships could sail closer to the wind and were ordered to go ahead. The rest stayed at anchor during Palm Sunday.

The Great Race

On Monday there was a favourable wind from the west-south-west. The seamen were up early to raise the anchors as soon as the tide was in their favour. The *Mary Rose* started behind the pack, but Howard soon noted that she began to catch up with the others.

On Monday, the wind came west-south-west, which was very good for us, and we slept it not, for a the beginning of the flood we were under sail **[5]**... *slaking, where the* Kathrin Fortaleza *sailed very well … Your good ship, the flower, I trow, of all ships that ever sailed, reckoning … every ship and came within three spear length of the* Kathrin, *and spake to John [Flemming and] Peter Seman, and to Freman, master, to bear record that the* Mary Rose *did fetch her at the tai[l on her] best way and the* Mary's *worst way; and so, sir, within a mile sailing let her fly*

... at the stern **[6]**, and she all the other, saving five of six small ships which cut o[ver the] *Foreland* the next way. And, sir, then our course changed, and went hard upon a bowline **[7]** ... the *Foreland*, where the Mary Rose, *your noble ship, set the* Mary George, *the* Kathrin Prow, *a bark ... Lord Ferrers hired, , the* Leonard *of Dartmouth, and some of them were four mile behind m[e] or ever I came to the Foreland.* **[8]** *The next ship that was to me, but the* Sovereign, *was three mile behind ... but the* Sovereign *passed not half a mile behind me. Sir, she is the noblest ship of sail [of any] great ship, at this hour, that I trow be in Christendom.*

Towards the Downs

Sir, we had not been at anchor at the Foreland but the wind [turned] up at the Northerboard so strainably that we could ride no longer there without great danger **[9]** *[so] we weighed to get us to the Downs through the Gulls. And when we were in the midst, between the Brakes and the Goodwin, the wind veered out again to the west-south-west, where we were fain to make with your great ships three or four turns* **[11]**, *and God knoweth ... row channel at low water. As we took it, the* Sovereign *and the* Mary *stayed ... a quarter of a mile off the Goodwin Sands, and the* Maria de Loretta *offered her ... would none of it, and was fain to go about with a forewind back ... where she lyeth ... I fetched the Downs with many turns, and thanked be to God I ... Downs at anchor in fast.* **[12]**

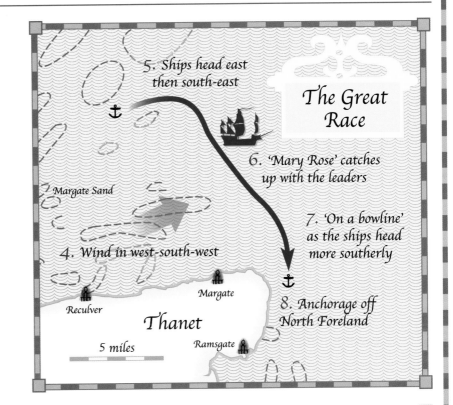

5. Ships head east then south-east

The Great Race

6. 'Mary Rose' catches up with the leaders

7. 'On a bowline' as the ships head more southerly

Margate Sand

4. Wind in west-south-west

Margate

8. Anchorage off North Foreland

Reculver

Thanet

5 miles

Ramsgate

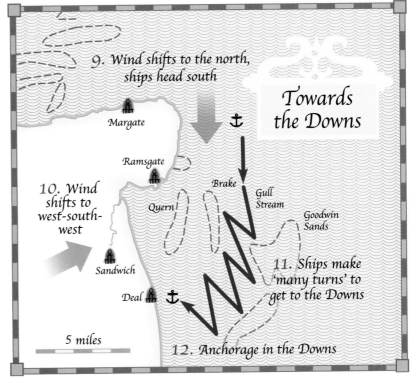

9. Wind shifts to the north, ships head south

Towards the Downs

Margate

Ramsgate

Brake

Gull Stream

Goodwin Sands

10. Wind shifts to west-south-west

Quern

Sandwich

11. Ships make 'many turns' to get to the Downs

Deal

5 miles

12. Anchorage in the Downs

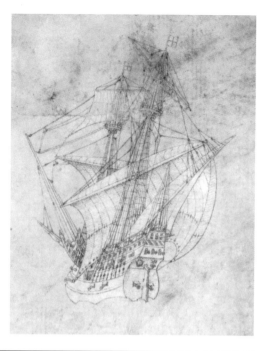

or 'on a bowline', as these ropes would now be tight on the windward side. To a 19th-century seaman it was a matter of great pride to keep the yards level; they were only angled, or canted, as a sign of mourning to symbolise the distress, and hence the negligence of the crew. But if the drawings on maps are to be believed, it was very different in the *Mary Rose*'s day. One of the ships shown in a map of Calais by Thomas Peyt shows a ship sailing close to the wind and has both fore and main yards at a distinct angle from the horizontal. Another had the main yard canted but the fore yard apparently level, perhaps to spread the foot of the topsail. Other drawings, for example the French off Brighton and Laurence Nowell's map of 1564, also show the yards canted to a greater or lesser degree. This might have partly compensated for the amount of bag in the sail, for it presented a straighter line, the yard, to the wind for part of its height. In effect it was being used almost as a lateen sail.

To move into the wind the ship had to pursue a zigzag course known as 'tacking' – although most navigators would rather wait for a favourable wind or tide. Each individual turn through the wind was also known as a tack. The ship was pointed into the wind, the foresail was used to push the bow round, while the after sails were brought over to the other side. When the wind was on the new side of the ship the foresails were also braced round and the ship settled on its new course. This was probably how the ship made 'many turns' off the Goodwin Sands in March 1513. Tacking could be difficult in rough seas and then the ship would wear by turning the stern towards the wind, which was slower but safer.

Steering

A little is known about how the *Mary Rose* was steered. The lower part of the rudder has survived, along with what appears to be the complete tiller. It is 3m long with a curve,

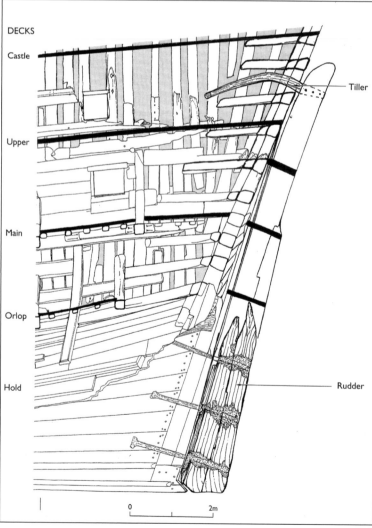

DECKS

Castle

Upper

Main

Orlop

Hold

Tiller

Rudder

0   2m

LEFT A reconstruction of the stern of the ship, showing how the rudder might have looked. The straight sternpost was essential so that the rudder could be hinged in more than two places. Three have actually been recovered, three more were probably needed.

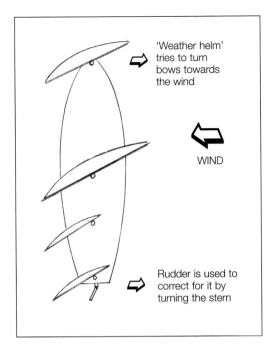

'Weather helm' tries to turn bows towards the wind

WIND

Rudder is used to correct for it by turning the stern

LEFT The effects of weather helm. If the sails are set normally the wind will tend to push the bows towards the wind, which can be corrected by the helm – if weather helm is excessive, then adjustments need to be made to the sails.

RIGHT The tiller of the *Mary Rose,* curved upwards and then downwards, which perhaps allowed men of different heights to operate it, either singly or together in strong winds. There is no clear sign of any attachment at the end, for either a whipstaff or steering wheel.

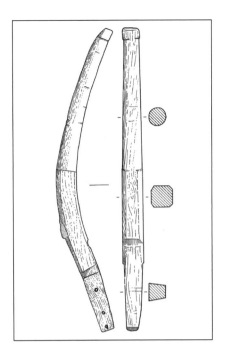

presumably upwards, of a metre. According to the Anthony Roll it was fitted aft on the upper deck. The steering wheel was nearly two centuries in the future at that time, and there is no sign of any fitting for the whipstaff, which would be used to extend the tiller in the next century. If fitted as conjectured, it would have had its outer end perhaps a metre above the deck with the curved section higher, which perhaps would have allowed several men to operate it at once. A tackle could have been fitted to its forward end to help in strong winds, but it was short compared with the tiller of HMS *Victory*, for example, which is nearly 9m long.

Steering a sailing ship depends on a certain amount of imbalance. Unless the wind is directly behind, the ship will probably bear 'weather helm'; that is, tend to head into the wind unless it is corrected by the rudder. The master would probably balance the sails so that weather helm was minimal, and the rudder was only needed for more precise steering. With his position below decks, the helmsman would have no view of what was going on outside. He might have a compass to steer by, but if the ship was sailing at an object or another ship, or it was necessary to keep the sails filled when close-hauled, then orders would have to be shouted down from the deck above. That was probably the job of the quartermasters.

Decoration and flags

There was very little carving on Henry VIII's ships, and even the figurehead had not yet emerged as the symbol of a ship. Paint was the main decoration of the hull, and according to the Anthony Roll the *Mary Rose* had a band of red and gold diagonal stripes on the sides of the fore- and aftercastles.

Flags and ceremonial made up for the plainness of the hull itself. When the *Great Harry* was new in 1514, an amazing set of flags,

BELOW The flags carried by one of the ships drawn off Calais, *c*1540. There are various Tudor symbols including the rose, the royal coat of arms with the lions of England and the lilies of France, a portcullis and a white feather. *(British Library)*

ABOVE A compass from the *Mary Rose*, missing the paper card or compass rose, which would have been marked with the 32 points. It is fitted on gimbals so that it would remain level in all circumstances.

ABOVE RIGHT A log reel recovered from the wreck.

banners and streamers was ordered, including emblems of all the places Henry associated himself with, such as England, Wales, Cornwall, Guienne and Spain. There were streamers up to 50yd long, some decorated in gold and bearing emblems such as dragons and the roses of the Tudors. The decorations of the *Mary Rose* were probably not much less elaborate when she was the newest and biggest ship in the navy four years earlier. By 1545, according to Anthony Anthony, she carried a long green and white streamer from each mast along with flags bearing the St George's cross. There was a royal standard at the masthead, a Tudor rose on the uppermost foredeck just above the bowsprit and several more along the sides, interspersed with other emblems.

Navigation

The *Mary Rose* was not intended to venture very far from shore, so sophisticated astral navigation techniques were not often needed and no instruments for it have been found in the wreck. According to William Bourne, navigators who took sights on celestial bodies were mocked as 'star shooters' and 'sun shooters' and were asked sarcastically if they had hit their

target. Apart from that the navigator used three main navigational instruments. The best known was the compass, first noticed in European ships in 1187. Three were found in the wreck, all small and stowed in chests, so they were not the ones being used for navigation at the time of the sinking. Essentially the compass was a magnetised needle that pointed towards magnetic north. Navigators were aware that this was not the same as true north, but did not have adequate means to correct for it. The needle was fixed on a pivot under a circular compass card, marked with the 32 points of the compass. This was fixed on gimbals inside a brass bowl within a wooden box. There is no sign of any structure such as a binnacle to hold a compass in place.

Speed was measured with a log line, which was run out from a reel, and one of these has been recovered. The time might be measured by sandglass and four of these were found. William Bourne suggested a different method. The navigator should recite 'some number of words', perhaps a favourite quotation or poem, to give the time. The advantage was that he could repeat it if the log ran out slowly, or cut it short if the ship was going fast.

The third instrument, and perhaps the most

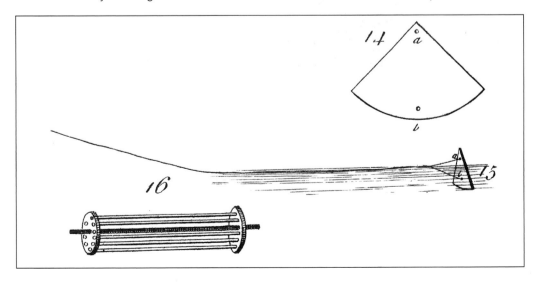

LEFT Details of the
log reel.

20cm

important, was the lead line, which could be used to warn of approaching shallows, and might help to indicate the ship's position. The navigator knew of the existence of various sandbanks, especially in the Thames Estuary, and the lead would indicate where he was in relation to them. Moreover, the lead was 'armed' with tallow in the hollow in its base. It would pick up a sample of the seabed, which would give the navigator much information. According to Bourne, if sailing east up the Channel: 'When you be nigh to Portland 30 fathoms, and stones like beans, and this sounding will last till St Alban's, or of the Isle of Wight, two or three leagues from the Isle of Wight, and you shall find 25 fathoms, with dents and clefts in the tallow like small threads.'

Charts, usually known as 'cards' or 'plats' were drawn on paper or vellum. They were known but were not common at the time. William Bourne wrote in 1580: 'I have known within these 20 years that them that was ancient masters of ships hath derided and mocked them that have occupied their cards

LEFT The principle of
the log and reel from
Falconer's *Marine
Dictionary* of 1769. By
that time the log was
shaped like a sector
of a circle. It was
dropped in the water
as at 15, and the line
attached to it ran out
on the reel.

LEFT Different sizes of leads from the *Mary Rose*. A hollow in the base was used for 'arming' it with tallow to pick up a sample of the sea bottom, which could help to establish the position, and also show whether the site was suitable for anchoring. The central one does not have the hollow while the nearest one is rather small and is perhaps used in shallower water.

CENTRE Dividers used for measuring off distances. The curved parts at the tops allow them to be opened and closed single-handed so that the navigator can steady himself or carry out other tasks.

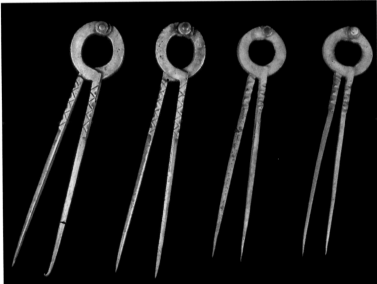

and plats … saying they care not for their sheep skins, for he could keep a better account upon a board.' But as a flagship the *Mary Rose* would have had the latest and best equipment. Charts would not be expected to survive centuries underwater, but four pairs of dividers have been found, suggesting that charts were used in some form.

Pilots

E ven the most experienced master could not be expected to know every place the ship might go, and he would hire a local pilot, or lodesman, where necessary. In May 1514 John Wodlas asked for payment for conveying the *Mary Rose* out of Harwich 'over a danger in the sea called the Naze' and taking her back again when the order was countermanded. Five days later he took her out once more 'through a place in the sea called the Slade' to meet the king, who was coming from Calais. Then he guided her through the Black Deeps into the Thames Estuary. The whole expedition took three weeks, and he had three men and a boat to assist him – either to take him to and from the ship he was piloting, or to sail ahead and find the depths of water. Pilots were not always available, especially off an enemy coast. During

Blanchief

LEFT The view of Beachy Head as seen from the west, a familiar and prominent sight to seamen navigating the south coast of England, as portrayed in the French *Grand Routier*.

the attack on Brest in April 1513, it is reported that the *Nicholas of Hampton* under Captain Arthur Plantagenet 'fell upon a blind rock, and burst asunder'. This served as a warning to the other ships, but it was an expensive way to find hazards, and the English captains saw that as 'the haven was dangerous to enter without an expert lodesman, they cast about and returned to their harbour'.

When crossing a sea such as the English Channel, which might be up to 100 miles wide, even the best navigator was not certain to arrive at exactly the point he wanted, and his first sight of land, the 'landfall' was important. A few years later William Bourne wrote: 'And the chiefest thing that belongeth to a seafaring man, is to know the place that he shall happen to fall with, which thing he must know by the beholding of the country, by taking some principal mark thereof.' The French edition of the *Routier* provided caricature-like images of various points along the coast, such as Beachy Head and Portland on the English side of the Channel.

Coming to anchor

Sail would be reduced towards the end of the voyage, or earlier if the wind got up. Illustrations of the time rarely show sails being furled; perhaps artists were much more interested in showing the drama of ships setting off on a voyage, or in full sail. It is significant that none of the inventories mention ropes such as clew lines, buntlines and so on, which were used in a later age to haul up a sail. We can only conclude that sails were lowered for furling on the decks or in the tops. This is consistent with the idea of bonnets, which were obviously handled from the bottom of the sail. Ropes known as martnets, attached to the edges of the sail by crow's feet, appear in later paintings and inventories of the 1540s.

A pilot would select an anchorage according to the depth of water, usually not more than 40 fathoms or 120ft. The nature of the seabed was considered – sand, mud and gravel were preferred, rock was to be avoided – as well as the strength of the current and the shelter from the prevailing winds. The anchor was prepared to drop, then let go as the ship moved backwards and cable was paid out. For the anchor to hold properly, the length of cable let out was usually three times the depth of water. Once secured in the anchor berth, the ship's three boats – the great boat, the cock and the jollyboat – were the main means of communication with the shore and with other ships.

Chapter Five

Fighting the Mary Rose

The *Mary Rose* carried a great variety of guns, which were added to during her years of service. Many of these, and the equipment associated with them, have been recovered from the wreck, throwing light on how guns were made and used in action. Other weapons, such as longbows, give unique insight into practices of the time.

OPPOSITE Main deck guns – a bronze muzzle-loader (foreground) with a pair of breech-loading iron guns behind. In addition to breech-loading wrought-iron guns, the *Mary Rose* carried a formidable array of muzzle-loading bronze guns, capable of shooting cast iron shot at 504 metres per second at long range. These guns rested on wheeled wooden carriages situated at gun bays with lidded gunports, a type of carriage which remained in use for the next 300 years. *(Courtesy Hufton & Crow)*

99

FIGHTING THE MARY ROSE

The ship of war

The *Mary Rose* was built as a warship, but unlike a rowing galley she was not radically different from ordinary merchant ships that could be taken up for the king's navy in wartime. Only her size and the extent of her armaments distinguished her. The main aim of a fleet was to land an invasion force or defend against one, or to protect one's own trade and attack that of the enemy. Battle was generally avoided if possible (although the fight off Brest in 1514 might be considered an exception), and the great guns and other weapons served mainly as a deterrent. If battle was joined, it was usually settled by boarding and capturing enemy ships. Heavy guns were only an aid to this, yet they increased in importance visibly during the *Mary Rose*'s life.

Guns were used on land in the defence of Florence in 1326, and were mounted on board ships by the time of the Battle of Sluys between the English and the French in 1340, but they were light anti-personnel weapons firing over the gunwales. The idea of cutting gunports in the sides is said to have come from a Breton with the suspiciously apt name of Descharge around 1500, in which case they were very new when the *Mary Rose* was conceived in 1509. This meant that much heavier guns could be mounted, even if only in small numbers for the moment. These guns could not be provided as personal weapons of the fighting men themselves, as medieval arms usually were, but had to be made especially for the king, increasing his power and partly causing what became known as 'the Tudor revolution in government'. Although they were rarely used in action, ships' guns had a profound effect on naval warfare and on society.

The early guns

Like most large ships of the day, the *Mary Rose* carried a great variety of weapons –

firearms, swords, pikes and bills and bows and arrows among others. The large carriage-mounted guns of the ship (that is, excluding handguns such as arquebuses) had a great variety themselves. These larger guns might be made in bronze or iron, cast in a mould or constructed in several pieces like a barrel; they might be muzzle or breech loading and mounted on several different types of carriage. The weight of shot varied from the 78lb (35kg) of a cannon-royal to 2½lb (1.134kg) for falcons, the smallest bronze guns listed. The idea of a single calibre for each type of gun was only just being established. The latest handguns were known as calivers, a corruption of calibre, because they had a uniform bore and size of shot. Amid the great variety, three main sizes can be identified. According to the *Complaint of Scotland* the heavy guns, the cannons, made a 'hideous crack' with the sound of 'duf, duf'. The medium-sized guns, the bases and falcons, sounded like 'tirduf, tirduf', while the others 'cryit tik tak tik tak'.

The *Mary Rose*'s earliest guns are listed in the inventory of 1514. It is often difficult to interpret, as some of the gun types are hard to identify, and the definitions were unclear even to contemporaries. These were largely based on shot type rather than size. There were several types of 'murderer', which fired small items as anti-personnel shot, although the single 'great murderer' may have had an anti-ship role. Two of these gun types were cast in brass, three others were of iron. They were breech loading, which implies they could be loaded from inboard without the need to let them recoil or run in for reloading, but suggests that their charge was relatively weak. 'Stone guns' were clearly defined by their role and there were 26 of these, the largest number present except the 28 'serpentines', which were long and thin, firing lead or iron shot. The most clearly defined weapons were the 'falcons' and 'falconets', which were small cast-bronze muzzle loaders with a clear anti-personnel role. The only large guns were those described as 'great'. There were five of these, all cast in brass, muzzle-loading and presumably firing shots of at least 34lb or 15.4kg. It is likely that two of them were arranged to fire from the lower deck through the stern, as heavy guns are almost invariably seen in that position in pictures of the day. The other three, plus the great murderer, may have been mounted to fire through gunports on the main deck, but that is by no means certain, and it is not known which of the ports had been cut by that time. The great majority of her 78 guns were light and for anti-personnel use.

BELOW LEFT A bronze cannon mounted through a gunport on the reconstruction of part of the main deck in the old Mary Rose Museum. Lids like the one shown were essential in keeping out water when the ship was in rough weather or heeling, and failure to close them in time probably contributed to the loss of the ship.

BELOW A gunport as seen from inside the ship. It is quite small, with little room to traverse the gun from side to side or elevate it up and down.

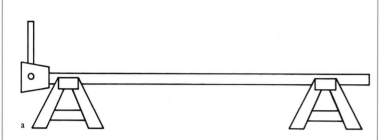

Making the mandrel that forms the core of the finished gun.

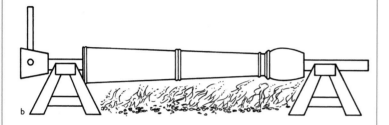

Making the wooden pattern in wood perhaps covered with clay. It includes a feeding head or reservoir to the right of the drawing, which would pressurise the molten liquid but not form part of the finished gun. The pattern is being dried over a fire.

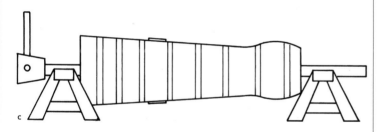

The mandrel and pattern are encased in a clay mould, which is then broken apart – because of this, each gun was unique.

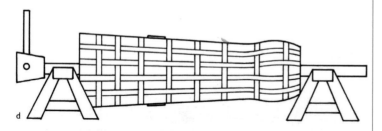

The final version of the clay mould, which is reinforced and will be turned vertically and filled with molten metal.

By 1545 the *Mary Rose* had a much more effective and sophisticated gun armament. The terminology had evolved, and the guns that have been recovered can mostly be matched with the Anthony Roll and other documents. There were much clearer roles for breech- and muzzle-loading guns, and for those of brass and iron.

Casting guns

By that time the heaviest guns were cast in bronze. They were expensive items, each with its individual character and highly decorated. They were known as brass guns to contemporaries but the alloy, of around 90% copper plus tin and other elements, was essentially bronze in modern terms. It survives well underwater and ten of the fifteen bronze guns listed by Anthony Anthony have survived, four recovered in the 19th century and the rest in the 20th.

The *Mary Rose*'s brass guns were made by the Arcana family at their foundry in London or by Peter Baude and the brothers John and Robert Owen in Houndsditch near the city. All were quite new, made between 1535 and 1543. Each cast gun originated in a wooden pattern that could not be reused, so every gun was unique. The pattern was made to the exact shape of the gun, including the elaborate decorations. This was put inside a jacket of clay reinforced with iron, which formed the female mould. That was broken open to remove the pattern, then reassembled. It was placed vertically in the ground with an iron rod to form the bore. Bronze was poured between the jacket and the rod to mould the gun.

Starting from the rearmost part, each gun had a cascabel button, which had not yet evolved into the ball shape of later years, but had an elaborate moulding. Then came the widest part, the base ring, followed by an area known as the reinforce, or first reinforce if there was more than one. It included the vent hole to light the powder, and a royal coat of arms. It had the thickest metal, for it was where the powder would explode. The external cross section of the gun was not necessarily circular, some were 'faceted' – 12- or 16-sided – for much of their length. The second reinforce continued the tapering of the barrel and it contained highly decorated dolphins or lifting

RIGHT The parts of a cast bronze gun. The rings are perhaps relics of the time when guns were made like barrels. Like most cast guns it tapers away from the breech, where the explosion of the powder will create the greatest stress.

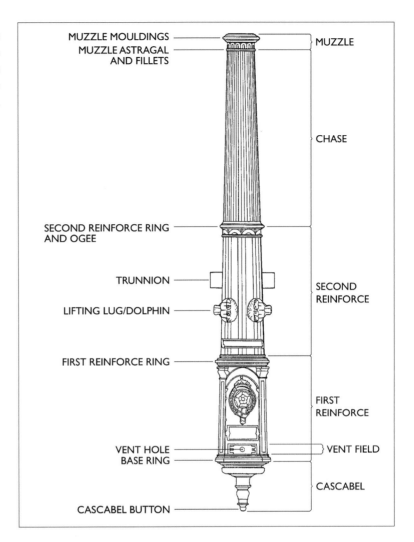

MUZZLE MOULDINGS
MUZZLE ASTRAGAL AND FILLETS
MUZZLE
CHASE
SECOND REINFORCE RING AND OGEE
TRUNNION
LIFTING LUG/DOLPHIN
SECOND REINFORCE
FIRST REINFORCE RING
FIRST REINFORCE
VENT HOLE
BASE RING
VENT FIELD
CASCABEL
CASCABEL BUTTON

lugs above. Just under the centre line were the trunnions on which the gun would pivot, placed a little to the rear of the centre for balance, because the metal was heavier at the breech. The chase continued the taper towards the muzzle. The areas were separated by decorative rings known as reinforce rings, with the muzzle astragal at the foremost part. Perhaps they had originated in the practice of making a gun like a cask, but they served no practical function in these guns. Internally the bore was usually parallel-sided and was slightly greater than the diameter of the shot intended for it.

Bronze guns

The bronze guns came in many different sizes. The largest on the *Mary Rose* was a single cannon-royal made by English founders the Owen brothers, yet possibly in France, in 1535. It had a bore of 8½in, which meant an iron ball of around 78lb – but like most of the recovered shot it was corroded and its weight reduced to 68lb. It was obviously very heavy for a man to

LEFT Details of a demi-cannon and its decoration, including an inscription stating that it was made by Robert and John Owen, a dedication to the king and the Tudor rose inside the motto of the Order of the Garter. *(Courtesy Stephen Foote)*

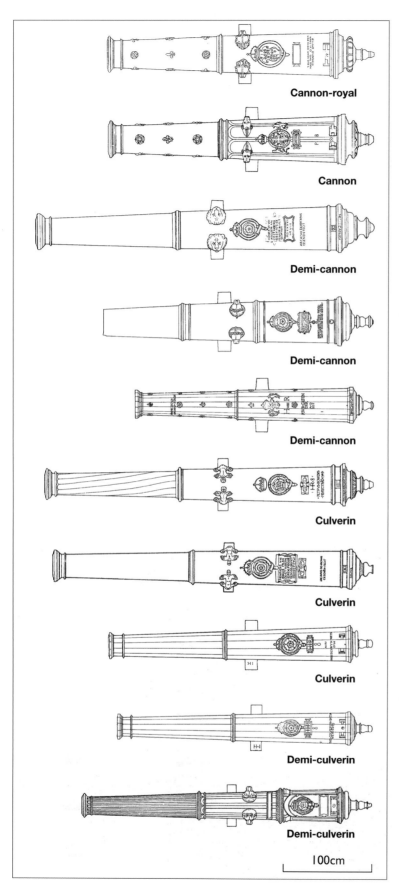

Cannon-royal

Cannon

Demi-cannon

Demi-cannon

Demi-cannon

Culverin

Culverin

Culverin

Demi-culverin

Demi-culverin

100cm

LEFT The bronze guns recovered from the *Mary Rose.* Different styles of decoration are apparent, including some of the culverins, which are wholly or partly fluted, while one has a spiral. Culverins are much longer than cannon in proportion to their bores.

handle in action. It was very short for its bore; the barrel was only 12 calibres long – that is, the bore was as long as 12 shots. Another cannon had a bore of 8in and therefore a ball of 68lb. A demi-cannon, such as the one made in England in 1542 and recovered in 1981, had a bore of 6½in. Its weight of shot was 32lb, although probably 34lb before corrosion took effect. In a sense it was a direct ancestor of the 32-pounders that dominated at the Battle of Trafalgar. The three demi-cannons found varied in length, from 15 to 21 calibres.

BELOW A selection of bronze guns, including a culverin, demi-culverin, demi-cannon and demi-culverin. The greater weight of the demi-cannon is obvious.

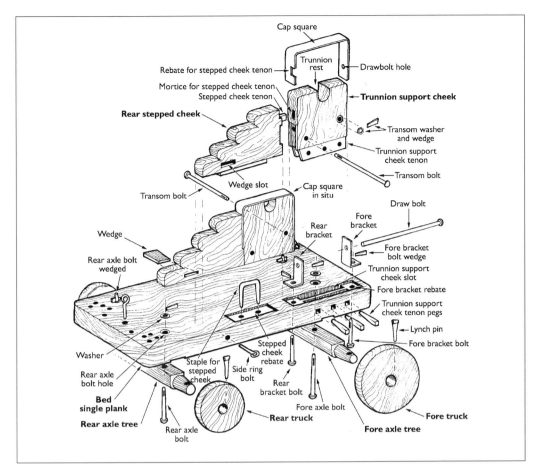

Cap square

Trunnion rest

Rebate for stepped cheek tenon

Drawbolt hole

Mortice for stepped cheek tenon
Stepped cheek tenon

Trunnion support cheek

Rear stepped cheek

Transom washer and wedge

Trunnion support cheek tenon

Transom bolt

Wedge slot

Cap square in situ

Transom bolt

Draw bolt

Wedge

Fore bracket

Rear bracket

Rear axle bolt wedged

Rear axle bolt wedged

Fore bracket bolt wedge

Trunnion support cheek slot

Fore bracket rebate

Trunnion support cheek tenon pegs

Lynch pin

Fore bracket bolt

Washer

Stepped cheek rebate

Rear axle bolt hole

Staple for stepped cheek

Side ring bolt

Rear bracket bolt

Fore bracket bolt

Bed single plank

Fore axle bolt

Fore truck

Rear axle tree

Rear axle bolt

Rear truck

Fore axle tree

LEFT The parts of a gun carriage as reconstructed from pieces found in the wreck. It is based on a solid wooden bed and with cheeks to support the trunnions of the gun, and stepped cheeks behind them to help cope with the recoil.

These were the heavy guns. The next in size were the culverins, which were also cast in brass and muzzle-loaded. They had smaller bore than the cannon but greater length. According to the lists of the time they might be up to 35 calibres long, but those of the *Mary Rose* varied from 19 to 26 calibres. The largest ones, the whole culverins, fired a ball of 20lb; the demi-culverins fired a shot of just under 10lb. The ship was supposed to carry two full culverins, but in fact four were recovered, including one of a rather ambiguous size. There were 6 demi-culverins, but only 2 were recovered. The sakers were the next largest guns but only two of these were listed, along with a single falcon. The sakers fired balls of 4lb 12oz, the falcon 1½ to 2½lb. An even smaller gun, the falconet, fired a ball of 1¾lb.

The bronze guns were mounted on what became known as truck carriages, so called after the small wooden wheels that supported them. This would have allowed the gun to recoil or be run in and out for reloading for firing, yet there is no sign that this was done at the time. It might also permit a gun to be moved

from one port to another, but the heights of the ports varied and so did the carriages, so each was probably tailored to an individual gun in a particular port. The base of each carriage was a bed made from one or two planks. Underneath

BELOW A reproduction culverin being loaded, with a rammer and other implements laid out and a stout breech rope that will restrain its recoil. Alexzandra Hildred stands behind the gun to the right.

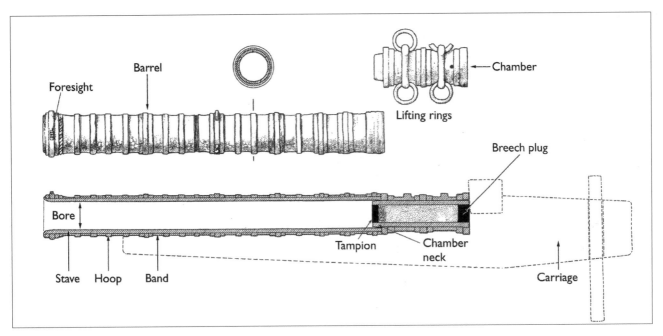

ABOVE The parts of a wrought-iron gun, showing the barrel-like construction of the barrel and how it is held together by rings. It also shows the separate chamber and the outline of the solid wooden carriage.

it, or occasionally above it, the trucks were attached to the ends of wooden axle trees. Above, each of the gun's trunnions was supported by a rectangular wooden cheek and held in place by a metal cap square. Behind that was a stepped cheek as a brace against the recoil of the gun.

The *Mary Rose* had eight port pieces when she sank. Most iron guns were wrought rather than cast, and each was made up of a number of pieces rather like a cask – hence the term 'barrel'. Wrought-iron guns were also breech- rather than muzzle-loading. Each had a pair of chambers to be wedged at the rear of the gun, so that one could be loaded while the other was being fired. Metalworking was

not precise in those days and a wrought-iron gun was likely to leak or even explode if it was overcharged with powder, while the wedge might fly out if not fixed firmly.

The port pieces were the most numerous carriage-mounted iron guns, with 12 listed on the Anthony Roll, of which 8 were recovered. They were breech-loading iron guns firing stone or 'murthering' shot. They also fired lantern shot, small pieces of stone shrapnel in lantern-shaped canisters. Externally, their sides were more or less parallel except where the rings held them together. They varied in bore diameter from 6in to 7¾in, which made them as big as cannons. Since their shot was made of stone it is difficult to equate with weight with those of iron shot,

RIGHT Making a reproduction port piece in 1998.

RIGHT CENTRE Sizing a hoop over a specially constructed cone.

FAR RIGHT Forcing the red-hot hoop into place by hitting on a jumping block.

LEFT Photomontage of a reproduction port piece superimposed on to a photograph of the main deck, showing its low situation that was consistent with the technique of breech-loading, as it allowed room for access over the gun.

CENTRE The reproduction port piece on its solid, wheeled carriage, with space behind the barrel for the chamber. It will be held in its place on the carriage by the solid timber behind it.

BELOW LEFT AND RIGHT Four men lifting the breech chamber as it would probably have been done during the *Mary Rose*'s lifetime, showing the use of the rings, and putting it in place behind the barrel. Wedges were needed to make it secure.

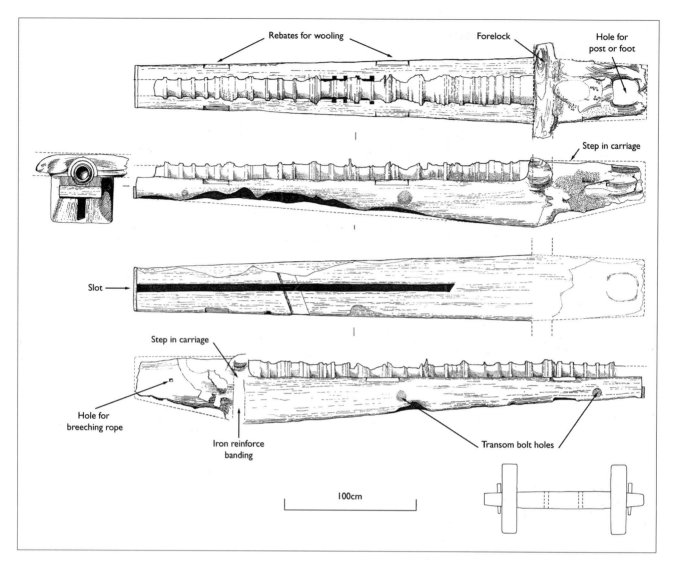

Rebates for wooling
Forelock
Hole for post or foot
Step in carriage
Slot
Step in carriage
Hole for breeching rope
Iron reinforce banding
Transom bolt holes

100cm

ABOVE A sling on its solid wooden carriage. The fore part of the barrel is missing in this case. With long bores, the slings are believed to be the wrought-iron equivalent to the bronze culverins.

RIGHT Fragments of possible fowlers, among the six recorded as being on board. Such guns are rare for the period, and their definition is not clear. They could fire stone and lead shot.

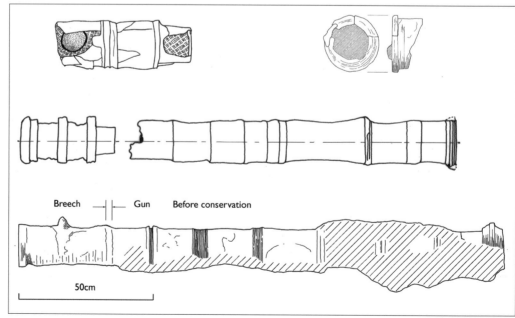

Breech
Gun
Before conservation

50cm

but each weighed up to 25lb. At least four of these guns were mounted on the starboard broadside of the main deck, with presumably the same number to port, so they formed part of the main armament of the ship. Two more may have been used as stern chasers, with another two possibly firing diagonally from the bow.

Iron breech-loading guns were mounted on a very different type of carriage, which fitted their method of operation. Each was based on a bed carved from a single piece of wood – basically a wedge hollowed out for the barrel and chamber and with a baulk behind the chamber. The barrel was lashed down and a wooden forelock and two iron folding wedges were inserted immediately behind the chamber to fix it in place. The whole assembly was on a pair of small solid wheels, or larger spoked wheels, with a moveable elevating post at the rear, to help aim the gun.

Two slings, three demi-slings and a quarter-sling were listed by Anthony Anthony and four of these have been recovered. In size the sling was equivalent to a saker, the demi-sling to a falcon and the quarter-sling to a falconet. They were the only iron guns that fired iron shot. Six iron 'fowlers' are listed on the Anthony Roll but they are difficult to identify either by archaeology or in the records. They may be a smaller version of the port piece, part of an attempt to rationalise the system of ordnance. Possible fowlers from the wreck have a bore length of up to 1,180mm and a diameter of 150–190mm. The smallest wrought-iron guns were the bases, each of which was fitted on the rail of the ship with a swivel. One could be aimed easily by a single man, with perhaps another to reload the spare chamber. Each was long and thin with a stock to fit in the gunner's shoulder. Some 30 of them were carried.

The idea of casting guns in iron was a relatively new one, although it offered the prospect of cheap mass production for the future. So far cast-iron guns were rare and mostly small, because it was difficult to guarantee the consistency of the iron and it had to be heated

to a very high temperature. However, the *Mary Rose* carried 20 and 4 have been recovered. They were known as hailshot pieces because of their ammunition. The bore was rectangular at its forward end. They were very small and on the boundary between handguns and fixed weapons. Each had a fin underneath. The gunner probably held its wooden stock in place under his armpit and rested the piece on a rail, which would absorb the recoil.

Gunpowder and shot

Gunpowder was first described in Europe by the English monk Roger Bacon in 1260. It is a mixture of 75% saltpetre, which provides oxygen, 15% charcoal, which provides fuel, and 10% sulphur, which speeds the combustion. The ingredients had to be mixed very carefully to give any kind of consistency to the product, for perhaps ten hours, and wetted during the process to prevent an accidental explosion. Gunpowder came in two main types in the early 16th century. Serpentine was the older version, simply a fine powder containing the three ingredients. With corn powder the compound was formed into small grains, which allowed air to circulate among them and increased the efficiency. The *Mary Rose* was listed as carrying two 'lasts' (a total of 4,800lb or 2,176kg) of serpentine powder, presumably in 24 barrels, along with 3 barrels of corned powder, which was perhaps used for handguns or for priming.

The *Mary Rose* carried a variety of different kinds of shot, not all of which are listed in the

ABOVE A base.

LEFT A hailshot piece. These were early examples of cast-iron guns, although they were very small and each was probably fired by one individual firing iron anti-personnel shot from an almost rectangular bore.

ABOVE Various types of shot including stone, round cast lead and round cast iron. Other types included spiked shot, composites of different metals and dice shot for hailshot, but round cast iron is by far the most common.

official inventories. The greatest quantity was of iron round shot, used by the bronze guns and the slings. Some 60 rounds of shot were provided for each falcon, suggesting a high rate of fire, whereas the larger guns usually had 25–30 rounds each. The slings and demi-slings had even less. A gap known as windage was left between the diameter of the shot and the bore to allow the shot to be inserted. Stone shot was used for the port pieces and fowlers, while the bases were loaded with composite lead shot with iron dice inside. They too had a low allocation of 13 rounds per gun, whereas handguns such as arquebuses were allowed 20 – presumably the bases would only be used during the immediate prelude to boarding, while the handguns could be used before and during the operation. Other types of shot included crossbar for use against the rigging and hailshot, which consisted of small cubical pieces of iron.

Gun operation

The muzzle-loading guns on the main deck of the *Mary Rose* must have been somewhat difficult to reload, as there was very little space to run them in to get access to the muzzle with room to fit a powder ladle, swab or rammer. Another possibility is that they were loaded from outboard, with a daring seaman perching on the barrel. This seems doubtful as there is no mention of it in the literature of the period, and it would undermine the purpose of having trucks on the carriage. It seems more likely that they were deliberately hauled in after firing. In 1578, William Bourne believed that great guns should be 'fast breeched' in battle, implying that they did not recoil. In view of the shortage of space, it

CENTRE Ladles and ladle heads for different types of gun. Ladles could be used to load the gun directly or to measure the amount of powder in a cartridge.

LEFT Possible sponges and rammers used for cleaning out the barrel and ramming home the shot. The sponge was used after firing, to remove any burning embers before reloading.

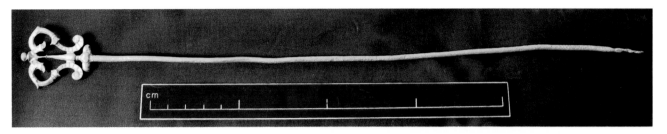

ABOVE Decorated copper alloy priming wire, pushed through the touch hole to prick the cartridge after loading to make it easier to ignite. Another of the gunners' characteristic tools and often decorated to his taste.

ABOVE The remains of a wad from a port piece chamber. They were only found in breech-loading guns, to keep the shot in place.

is possible that the guns were turned through up to 90° once they were inboard to allow access.

The first task was to clean the barrel, then load the gun with powder. This might be done using a ladle, although by 1578 Bourne was aware of the faults of this procedure and he recommended putting the powder in paper cartridges beforehand. There is evidence that these were used in the *Mary Rose* – 'formers' to make the shape of several different cartridges have been found, paper was listed even if not in evidence, and five priming wires to prick the cartridge through the touch hole have been discovered. But parts of many ladles were also found, for filling cartridges, or for inserting them into the gun, or for emergency use when cartridges ran out, or as part of the normal loading system. If the gun was loaded with loose powder it had to be rammed home tightly in the breech, then a wad of old rope was inserted to hold it in place. After that the ball or other shot was put in, with another wad to retain it. A small amount of powder from the gunner's dispenser was then let into the touch hole, and the gun was ready to fire as soon as a target was available.

The breech-loading guns posed fewer problems; it was quite simple to remove the forelock and wedges that secured the chamber and take it aside to reload it, while inserting another one and putting the shot in the rear of the barrel. With either breech- or muzzle-loading guns it was essential to make sure that there were no burning embers left in the chamber. With a breech-loading chamber it simply had to be washed, refilled with powder and sealed with a wooden plug or tampion; but with muzzle-loading it was necessary to put a sponge on the end of a pole to wash out the barrel, and use a worm to remove any fragments of cartridge or wad. Only then could the gun be reloaded.

Aiming

The guns could be traversed or pivoted to give a certain amount of flexibility in aim, although the narrowness of the gunports and the structure of the hull greatly restricted this in many places. Likewise the guns could be elevated and depressed to a limited extent, barely enough to counter the heel of the ship and keep the barrel level. The general rule was to let the target come within the range and bearing of the gun in question. Thus the gunner needed good cooperation with the helmsman, according to Bourne: 'He that is at the helm must be sure to steer steady, and be ruled by him that giveth the level, and he that giveth fire, must be nimble, and ready at a sudden.' On the *Mary Rose*, where the steering position was well below decks, a quartermaster would have to take these sights and have his orders transmitted to the helmsman, who was perhaps not too far away if the quartermaster was in the waist. Aiming also depended on the effects of the sea. After the first discharge it was apparently the custom to turn the ship round to fire the other broadside. Certainly this was common by the end of the century, and a survivor from the loss of the *Mary Rose* claimed that such an operation was in place when she sank. This is largely confirmed by archaeological evidence.

RIGHT **The reconstruction of the face of an archer, identified by the condition called 'os acromiale', which affected the shoulder blades and was caused by stress on the arm and shoulder muscles.** *(The Mary Rose Trust/Oscar Nilsson)*

FAR RIGHT **Reconstructed longbow chest with a selection of longbows from the 172 recovered. Some 7,834 arrow fragments (2,303 of which were complete arrows) were recovered of the 9,600 listed. They were still regarded as useful weapons in the early gunpowder age.**

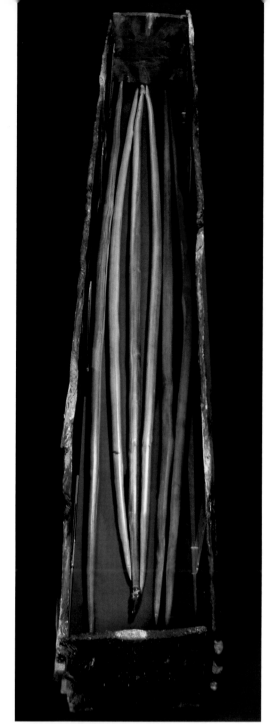

Personal weapons

Longbows were used in action at the battle between the *Regent* and *Cordelière* off Brest in 1512 and it was reported: 'Our men so valiantly acquit[ted] themselves that within one hour fight they had utterly vanquished with shot of guns and arrows the said carrack, and slain most part of the men with the same.' But they probably declined in importance over the decades. Some 250 longbows were listed for the *Mary Rose* in the Anthony Roll and 99 of these were found in two chests stowed on the orlop deck. Also, 50 handguns, probably of the arquebus type, were recorded in the Anthony Roll with 20 rounds of ammunition for each. Remains of 6 handguns were found, all towards the stern and all but one within the stern castle, suggesting that like the longbows they were ready for action. The stock of a possible pistol-

RIGHT **Part of an arrow bag containing arrows, including a leather spacer and strap. Spacers were used by the archers to keep the arrows apart and prevent damage to the flights.**

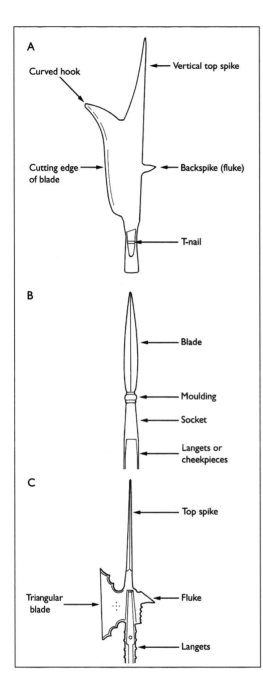

A
- Curved hook
- Vertical top spike
- Cutting edge of blade
- Backspike (fluke)
- T-nail

B
- Blade
- Moulding
- Socket
- Langets or cheekpieces

C
- Top spike
- Triangular blade
- Fluke
- Langets

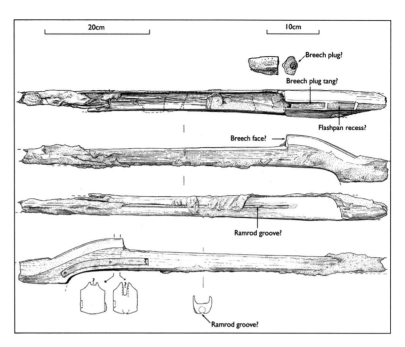

20cm
10cm
- Breech plug?
- Breech plug tang?
- Flashpan recess?
- Breech face?
- Ramrod groove?
- Ramrod groove?

ABOVE Parts of an arquebus or harquebus. Only fragments of stocks survive but they probably used the matchlock for firing, with a ramrod for loading through the muzzle.

LEFT A bill, defined by its hook and point; a pike, spear-like and with a much simpler shape; and a halberd with its axe-like head. Apart from a few fragments of heads, only the wooden staffs (or hafts) of such weapons survive, but pikes and bills are listed in the Anthony Roll.

BELOW The only surviving complete sword complete with its basket-hilt, which protects the hand of the user. None are listed in the inventories as they were the personal property of the users.

like weapon has been found, although the word was not yet in the English language.

The ship is listed as carrying 150 pikes, long-shafted weapons with pointed iron heads, and the same number of bills, with axe-like or hooked heads. These were obviously useful in repelling boarders and could cut the enemy rigging at close quarters, but they would be too clumsy for a man boarding an enemy ship to handle. Most of those found in the wreck were within the stern castle and the waist, suggesting that the ship was ready to repel boarders. The ship was issued with 480 'darts for tops'. If some of these were placed ready for action they would have been lost with the masts, but three large incendiary darts were found in the wreck. But several pictures of the period show spear-like weapons in tops, ready to drop on the deck below if the ship is boarded; and certainly that is something that was feared when the 1530 fleet orders were compiled. Swords and daggers were in common use by civilians as well as those conscripted for military service and they too would be useful in boarding or repelling boarders, as well as marking the social status of the owner.

Going into battle

Ships generally sailed in loose formation when not in contact with the enemy. It is not known what formation, if any, that Howard's ships adopted on going into action with the French in August 1512. Ideally ships sailed in line abreast when approaching the enemy, although that was probably not practicable in the narrow Channel and when rounding a headland, as in this case. Even at best, the line abreast formation was difficult to hold together with ships of many different sailing qualities, and there is no sign that fleets trained in the manoeuvre. It would be disrupted even further if ships had to turn one side to the enemy to fire their broadside guns.

The formation of 19 July 1545 (such as it was) was ad hoc and much affected by the light winds and the sudden arrival of the enemy. There is no discernible pattern in the ships shown in the Cowdray engraving, except that a few of the galleys seem to be near the front of the formation, which would only be natural as they would have left the harbour first when the wind was light; and there is a distinct tail of ships still coming out of the harbour. The French fleet does not have much more order as it rounds the eastern end of the Isle of Wight in the same picture, but in that case the galleys have clearly gone ahead to lead the attack.

Lord Lisle's orders of 1545 were written just after the *Mary Rose* sank and may have been affected by that battle. However, they do show that tactical thinking had advanced some way since 1512. His fleet consisted of a vanguard of three ranks. The second rank was the most powerful and would have included the *Mary Rose* if she had not gone down a few weeks earlier. There were two wings consisting of galleys, which were always difficult to integrate with sailing ships. The three ranks of the main body were each to sail in line abreast and it was commanded that 'the ranks must keep such order in sailing that none impeach another. Wherefore it is requisite that every of the said ranks keep right way with another, and take such regard in observing the same that no ship pass his fellows forward nor backward nor slack anything but [keep] as they were in one line, that there may be half a cable length between every of the ships.'

The weather gage

On sighting the enemy, the most important action for an English fleet was to gain the weather gage – that is, to get to the windward side, 'by all means he can' according to the 1530 orders. If the fleet looked like losing the weather gage, one tactic was to pretend to flee. In theory the enemy would pursue until he was within range, when he would fire and the smoke from his guns would obscure his view of the English, who would then tack and gain the weather gage – although there is no evidence that this was ever tried in practice.

The weather gage would allow a fleet to control the tactics of the battle, to decide where and when to attack. Just as important, it meant that the copious smoke produced

BELOW **The English fleet shortly after the *Mary Rose* sank, showing a large ship – presumably the *Great Harry* – in the lead firing her bow guns and a variety of smaller vessels including ships and galleys behind, in no particular formation.**

First rank

Left oared wing

Second rank

Right oared wing

Third rank

ABOVE Sir Thomas Audley's orders for the English fleet in August 1545, just after the sinking of the *Mary Rose*, showing the sailing ships in regular order in the centre and the galleys forming the wings.

by the powder of the day would drift down on the enemy, perhaps choking him but at least obstructing his view. As the Spanish commander Alonso de Chaves put it:

If there be no other advantage he will always keep free from being blinded by the smoke of the guns, so as to be able to see one to another; and for the enemy it will be the contrary, because the smoke and fire of the fleet and of their own will keep driving upon them, and blinding them in such a manner that they will not be able to see one another, and will fight amongst themselves from not being able to recognise each other.

The fleet orders of around 1530 tried to counter this problem by making sure that the ships were clearly identified: 'The admiral ought to have this order before he joins battle with the enemy, that all his ships shall bear a flag in their mizzen tops, and himself one on the foremast beside the mainmast, that everyone may know his own fleet by that token.'

Attack and defence

The 1530 orders were probably based on long-established precedents, but might have incorporated the experience of the *Mary Rose* and *Regent*'s fight off Brest in 1513. Protocol was important; the flagship was to attack the enemy counterpart. According to Audley's orders: 'No private captain should board the admiral enemy but the admiral of the English, except he cannot come to the enemy.' Chaves did not want the flagship to grapple too soon, but to stand aside and control the action: 'The captain-general should never be the first who are to grapple nor should he enter the press, so that he may watch the fighting and bring succour where

it is most needed.' Apart from that, as stated in the 1530 orders, each ship was to pick out one nearest in size to itself: 'Let every ship match equally as near as they can, and leave some pinnaces at liberty to help the over matched.' One small ship was to be attached to the flagship to prevent it being overcome, which would be 'a great discouragement' to the other crews. Referencing Lisle's orders of 1545, the ships of the first two ranks were 'appointed to lay aboard the principal ships of the enemy, every man choosing his mate as they may, reserving the admiral or the lord high admiral'. In the 1530 orders, each of the attacking ships was to come alongside its opponent, wait until he had finished firing and the smoke had cleared, then 'shoot off all your pieces, your port-pieces, the pieces of hail-shot [and] cross-bow shot to beat his cage deck'. The captain was to see that the enemy decks were 'well ridden' or cleared and to try to deal with the darts and other weapons being dropped or fired from the enemy tops. Then he was to enter, or board, with his best men leading the way.

The aim of each ship was to grapple with one of the enemy, then board. Although it was always present as an aspiration, the *Mary Rose* never actually executed it, even in the Battle of Bertheaume Bay when she came closest. However, the fight between the *Regent* and *Cordelière* is described by Holinshed:

Sir Thomas Knyvet ... suddenly caused the Regent ... to make the carrack, and to grapple with her along board. And when they of the carrack perceived they could not depart, they let slip the anchor, and so with the stream the ship turned, and the carrack was on the weather side, and the Regent on the lee side. The fight was cruel between these two ships.

ABOVE The grapnel in the bows of the *Mary Rose* as depicted on the Anthony Roll. Only the largest ships – the *Great Harry, Mary Rose* and *Peter Pomegranate* – are recorded as being fitted with them. *(Pepys Library, Magdalene College, Cambridge)*

BELOW A grapnel and other items recovered by the Deane brothers and since lost. It is not clear if the hook was used in battle or for anchoring boats.

In that case the two ships were clearly alongside one another, and lashed together with grappling irons. The tumblehome of the two ships would have made boarding difficult, but there was another way to attack. The Anthony Roll shows the *Mary Rose*, like the *Great Harry* and *Peter Pomegranate*, with a grapnel hanging from the bowsprit in the furthest forward position that was possible. It is not likely that it would be needed as an anchor in such a position, so it was presumably to be used in grappling another ship for boarding. This implies that the ship might attack by putting its bow across the enemy hull. The forecastle offered a bridge for this, but it had its dangers. The *Mary Rose* herself was well armed with guns firing into the waist to repel just such an attack.

When boarding, according to the 1530 orders, each captain was to make sure that the enemy was already suffering, that his decks were 'well ridden' or cleared. He should try to silence the enemy's tops, from which men might fire guns or drop spears and darts. He was to board or 'enter' with his best men. If another enemy ship came to the rescue he was to 'bulge' or scuttle the ship under attack, making sure that his own men had retreated, taking the enemy captain prisoner and leaving the rest of the crew to be 'committed to the sea'.

Galleys presented different problems. The *Mary Rose* first came up against them in the battle off Brest in 1513, although it is not certain that she was actually engaged. Her final

conflict in July 1545 was largely directed against some of the 25 French galleys that entered the Solent. Galleys were only successful in perfect weather conditions, but with them they had an ideal combination of fire and movement that could be devastating, and they had them on these two occasions. The answer in the latter confrontation was for the *Mary Rose* and other leading ships to approach them, fire broadsides and turn away. It seems that neither side did any real damage to the other, and the capsize of the *Mary Rose* was probably due to accident rather than enemy action.

Apart from assisting at the guns or using other weapons, the soldiers on board might form landing parties as marines did in later ages. The *Mary Rose* saw more of this kind of action than any other. In April 1513 Howard got about 1,500 men from the fleet into ships' boats, but the French force near Brest was too strong. Instead, they landed at Crozon across the harbour. Later in the month the troops were crammed into small victualling ships – which had shallower draughts than the warships – for an attack on the French galleys on the shore, but were foiled by the arrival of the main enemy fleet offshore, which led to Howard's rash attack and death. In July 1522 the ships landed men and guns for a raid on Morlaix. However, the death of Howard at Blanc-Sablon was a warning, and the orders of 1530 demanded that an admiral should call his captains to a council of war before landing. If he ignored their advice,

even success would not bring a reward. In such a case, 'the king ought to put him out of his room for purposing a matter of such charge of his own brain, whereby the whole fleet might fall into the hands of the enemy to the destruction of the king's people'. This was rather different from the spirit of Nelson, in which disobedience, or proverbially turning a blind eye, would be rewarded if it led to victory.

In other ways some features of the *Mary Rose* did point towards the future. She did carry heavy muzzle-loading guns and iron guns as the navy would do two centuries later, but they were not the same; the large muzzle-loading guns were all bronze and their crucial role may have been recognised, but was not yet established. In fact naval tactics would go through at least two stages before the line of battle, the classic English disposition, was evolved. More forward-firing guns were added during the 50 years after the *Mary Rose* sank, and the underwater shape of the bows redesigned to cope with them. By 1617 Sir Henry Mainwaring was able to write: 'A man of war pretends to fight most with his prow.' The next stage came soon afterwards, as ships got longer and larger and more guns were secured to the broadside, while loading techniques allowed much more rapid fire without turning or withdrawing from the action. This led to the line of battle as first used by the English in 1653 and marked the beginning of British naval supremacy. But no one could have predicted that in 1545 as the *Mary Rose* fought her last battle.

BELOW French galleys in the Solent, 19 July 1545, showing their manoeuvrability against the wind, and their forward-firing armament.

Chapter Six

Recovering the Mary Rose

From the first days after her sinking, the wreck of the *Mary Rose* inspired the use of innovative underwater techniques including some of the first diving helmets. In the 20th century, the insight and determination of Alexander McKee and Margaret Rule was combined with the latest technology to find and recover the hull with the aid of a large team.

OPPOSITE The hull in its cradle soon after lifting showing the *Tog Mor*, with HRH the Prince of Wales's standard flying on the *Sleipner*, from which Christopher Dobbs took the photograph.

Early attempts

Plans for the recovery of the *Mary Rose* began almost immediately after her sinking. At the end of July 1545 the Duke of Suffolk wrote that 'we intend with all speed to set men in hand for that purpose'. Venetians were the salvage experts of the day and their Lagoon was shallow and tidal like the Solent. Thirty Venetian 'mariners', including divers and a carpenter, were hired, with 60 English sailors to assist them. The largest ships available, the *Jesus of Lubeck* and the *Sampson,* were made ready, along with another hulk. Ten new capstans were prepared, complete with pulleys. Rafts constructed of spare masts would also play a part, perhaps as bases for the workers.

The ship had settled on the seabed at an angle of 60°, with her masts still showing. Much of the rigging was removed and it was planned to attach cables to the masts to haul her upright, which would perhaps help free the hull from the silt. Hulks were placed on each side to help right her. She would be towed into shallow water at high tide, then the water drained or pumped out at low tide. This had been tried by 9 August, but failed. The French threat to the Solent receded by September but no progress was made. Peter Paule, a Venetian diver, was paid for retrieving some of the guns, but was sent to the Tower of London for attempting to desert. Even though an amount of £559 8s 7d was spent on the attempted recovery, the ship was finally left to rot on the seabed. Sir William Monson, who first went to sea in 1585, claimed that he had seen her timbers with his own eyes, but implied that they were no longer visible when he wrote in 1623. The port side of the hull was exposed to water, tide and the voracious shipworm, and it rotted away; much of the starboard side gradually sank in the mud and eventually was covered up. With the passing of time the ship was largely forgotten.

The Deane brothers

There was another great disaster in the Solent in 1782 when the 100-gun flagship *Royal George* foundered with the loss of around 1,000 lives, including many visiting women and children. Unlike the *Mary Rose* the wreck was a hazard to navigation in the shipping channel as well as an embarrassment, reminding viewers of a spectacular failure of British shipbuilding and seamanship. But it was more than half a century before the technology was available to do anything about it.

Charles Deane had designed a copper helmet fed by an air pump, which could be used for fire rescue, but he and his brother John soon found that it was even more valuable for diving. It offered far greater mobility, vision and underwater time than the diving bell that had been used for centuries. They worked near the small Kentish port of Whitstable, recovering lost equipment, and cleared an East Indiaman wreck off the Isle of Wight, and from 1832 they were lifting guns from the *Royal George* with Admiralty approval. They were asked to clear the wreck, and while doing this they were approached by 'five poor fishermen', presumably using the new technique of trawling, whose nets were constantly being fouled in a site to the north-east. In July 1836 John discovered a bronze demi-cannon clearly marked with Henry VIII's insignia and bearing the date 1542. It did not take long to establish that it could only have come from the *Mary Rose*. Over the next few years he retrieved more guns and many other objects on the seabed, exhibited them, and produced

BELOW Wreck of the *Royal George* at Spithead, 1782. *(©2000, Topham/ Picturepoint)*

detailed drawings. There was a good deal of public interest, and furniture was carved from the timber of the wreck. But Charles Deane, not the most stable of men, was committed to Peckham Lunatic Asylum for a time, and there were disputes with the government and with the fishermen over salvage rights. The enterprise reached the end of its natural life – any further investigation would require a great deal of underwater excavation, which was difficult if not impossible with the technology of the time.

The *Mary Rose* wreck was left, while the military engineer Sir Charles Pasley destroyed the *Royal George* with large quantities of explosives. Commander Sheringham of the Royal Navy included the wreck, along with that of the *Royal George*, on his chart of 1841 but that lay unnoticed in the archives for many years. There were no longer any objects protruding from the *Mary Rose* to disturb the fishermen, and meanwhile two myths gained prevalence. It was believed that the *Mary Rose* wreck had been discovered accidentally by Deane while diving on the *Royal George*. With the limitations of even their advanced equipment, that would have meant it was very close indeed. And Pasley's biographer suggested that he had dealt with the *Mary Rose* in the same way as the larger ship; that is, he had destroyed it by explosives. This was compounded by the fact that Deane had indeed

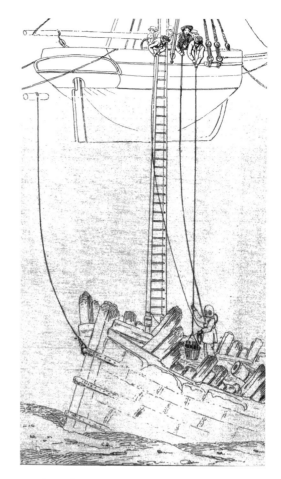

used small explosive charges to ease their excavation of the *Mary Rose*, although these had done little or no damage to the wreck. The common view was that the *Mary Rose* no longer existed.

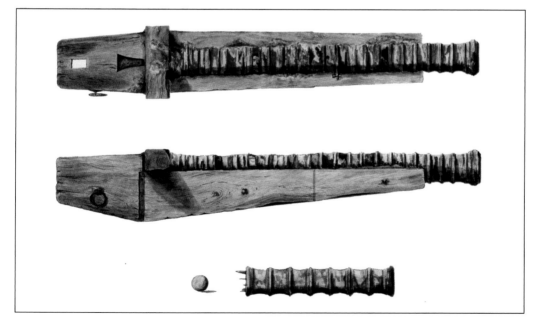

McKee and the rediscovery

By the 1960s human access to and knowledge of the underwater world had increased dramatically. Anti-submarine campaigns in two world wars had led to the development of the echo-sounding apparatus asdic, later known as sonar. It had been taken up by the oil industry for underwater exploration, and it was now possible to make a map of the seabed, including irregularities that might indicate a wreck. In 1943 Jacques Cousteau and Émile Gagnan invented the aqualung or self-contained underwater breathing apparatus (SCUBA), which allowed a diver complete freedom of movement in reasonably shallow water, such as the Solent. It was also much cheaper and needed less training than using the diving suit and helmet. Diving was now accessible to almost anyone who was moderately fit and could afford the equipment. The British Sub Aqua Club Diving Manual (first published in 1959) waxed lyrical about the underwater world:

The pleasure of diving is many-sided and as diverse as the feelings of those taking part. ... Each time a diver sinks below the surface his whole world changes: the light dims and colours fade as the sun's rays are rapidly absorbed by the water: normal hearing ceases, to be replaced by a vague awareness of slight sounds that cannot be located – sounds of sea creatures, stones rattling in the waves' thrust and surge, the gurgle of a demand valve. Taste and smell are non-existent and the feel of the water is all-encompassing.

But conditions in the Solent were not always so pleasant.

Alexander McKee was a military historian who had mainly written on the Second World War, but he had always been fascinated by the story of the *Mary Rose*. He was aware that plans, models and paintings were available for warships from about 1650 onwards, but much less was known about ships of a century or so earlier. He believed that the *Mary Rose* still existed somewhere under the Solent, and that it was 'the most important known wreck in North-West Europe' as a very early example of a purpose-built warship with lidded gunports. Until that point underwater archaeology had largely concentrated on the Mediterranean where Cousteau and Gagnan had developed the aqualung. Work was mainly on submerged harbours and cities, and the deep and rocky waters of the sea did little to conserve ship timbers. It was commonly believed that the strong tides around the British Isles would quickly destroy any wooden wreck. When a Swedish warship, the *Vasa* of 1628, was raised almost intact from Stockholm Harbour in 1961, the possibility of preservation in the less hospitable waters of northern Europe was raised. But still there was great scepticism about the survival of the *Mary Rose*, and several different sites were suggested for its position.

McKee began to explore the *Royal George* site in 1965, but he concealed his hopes about the *Mary Rose* from his colleagues in the local diving club, calling his project 'Solent Ships'. He took on the land archaeologist Margaret Rule as an adviser. Finding nothing from the Tudor age near the *Royal George,* he took bearings from

RIGHT Alexander McKee, the discoverer of the *Mary Rose,* wearing diving gear including a life jacket and carrying an underwater camera.

the Cowdray print, which suggested a different location, and he was aware that the king was said to have heard the cries of drowning sailors from near Southsea Castle – unlikely if the ship had foundered on the *Royal George* site. In 1966 he was shown the Sheringham chart of 1841 in the Royal Navy's Hydrographic Department. It gave the true position of the wreck, in six fathoms and half a mile from the *Royal George*; McKee's colleague John Towse gave an audible gasp when he spotted it. Then research in the Public Record Office told the real story of the Deanes' work on the *Mary Rose,* making it clear that it was not near the *Royal George* and had not been destroyed with it.

Money and equipment were both scarce but McKee got the loan of a side-scan sonar, as used by the oil industry. Up to then a nautical chart had usually been produced by taking spot depths either by a lead line or by echo-sounding, but the result was not nearly detailed enough to show the sort of irregularity that might indicate a wreck. A diver could only proceed very slowly in perhaps 10ft of visibility, but the side-scan sonar produced a map of the seabed up to 2,000ft wide – though

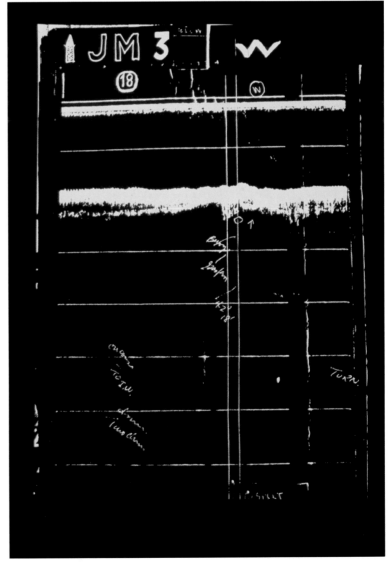

RIGHT Part of a sub-bottom sonar image, indicating the presence of a wreck. The rise and fall of the surface around the area of the vertical lines indicates the W-shape that a wreck might cause.

much less in shallower water. In August 1968 the archaeologists discovered a promising site, oval in shape and with the kind of flat W-shaped section in the sea bottom that might indicate the sides and decks of a wreck. In the meantime, McKee found a way of protecting the wreck from treasure hunters by leasing an area of the seabed from the Crown Estates, until the Protection of Wrecks Act was passed in 1973. Rods were sunk in the mud to try to give some indication of the shape of the wreck and water jets loaned by the local fire service cleared away some of the mud, while the project slowly gained support. In 1970 a gun, a wrought-iron sling, was found on the site. It was clearly Tudor in origin and the identity of the wreck was established. Now it attracted the support of Lord Mountbatten, who lived in the region, and his cousin the Duke of Edinburgh, who gave some support from his private funds. However, at a symposium in April 1971 it was suggested that the gun was merely ballast and that proved that only the bottom of the ship survived – which led to 'a rather angry exchange' according to McKee.

Water jets had been used to clear trenches on the site during 1969 and 1970, and there was much press interest when diving resumed in the spring of 1971. Percy Ackland dived

with McKee and nearly died when he vomited underwater. There was great difficulty in finding the previous year's trenches, but the divers persevered.

I headed S.W. for about 80 feet, when I noticed a change in the bottom. I swam back and found a ledge. I swam along the ledge and found a fragment of timber. I felt around it. It was not attached to anything.

I looked ahead and saw an indistinct dark object. It looked like a frame. IT WAS A FRAME! Eroded on top like a pyramid about two inches by ten inches. Six inches away was another one, and beyond that yet another.

They had found the *Mary Rose* at last.

The archaeology of the wreck

There was still a huge amount of work to be done just to survey and excavate the wreck, apart from any prospect of raising it. It was nearly all done by amateurs operating from small boats on the few days when the Solent tides and variable weather allowed diving. Perhaps the worst year was 1972, when according to McKee, operations had to be aborted on 59 out of 97 planned days. And when diving did take place, it was not pleasant:

Our suits stank from the clouds of macerated sewage that had swept across the site all week. Our muscles ached from holding on, to stop ourselves being hurled from one side of the boat to the other. Holding on, that is, for every second of eight hours. The time spent underwater might have been luxurious relaxation in comparison, had it not been for the bitter cold sea below and the chilling wind above. There was no way to get warm or rest this side of bed.

Originally the site was found each day by taking transits on landmarks. Even when a buoy was erected over the site there were hazards from shipping, including then Prime Minister Edward Heath who came close during a yacht race. Visibility varied from 3ft (1m) to 9ft, and occasionally 20ft. A typical dive was described by Geoffrey Morgan:

Underwater archaeology is rarely exciting, rather in my experience, consistently tedious. Sheer painstaking, meticulous toil. We carefully dug our trenches, measuring, drawing, noting important features, reporting every man-made find, including broken British Rail crockery from the many ferries which passed overhead. On returning the following day the tide would have filled up our trenches with weed, so the process would begin again. The labour was not unlike weeding a very large, untidy garden, without the pleasure of flowers or produce to show for one's efforts.

From 1971 the divers had the use of a 40ft catamaran named *Roger Grenville*, who at the time was believed to be the captain of the *Mary Rose*. Initially it had no motive power of its own and had to be towed out to the site, but it was equipped with an Atlas Copco compressor that powered the airlifts, suction devices used to remove spoil. In 1973 BP sold the project a redundant diving platform for £5, but it sank – McKee considered it 'the unparalleled opportunity to observe a re-run of the sinking of the *Mary Rose* herself'.

The main task was to establish the outline of the wreck by digging along the visible lines of timbers. The actual orientation of the wreck was still unknown and there was a certain amount of speculation. At one stage it was thought that the hull was probably preserved to a height of 9.1m (35ft 8in) above the keel at this point. Margaret Rule's hopes rose: 'If he was right, we had a British *Vasa*, intact to the upper deck. … If we could bring the hull into the sheltered

ABOVE Three of the boats used over the wreck site – the catamaran *Roger Grenville* used from 1975 to 1978, a diving safety boat and a fishing vessel provided by its owner.

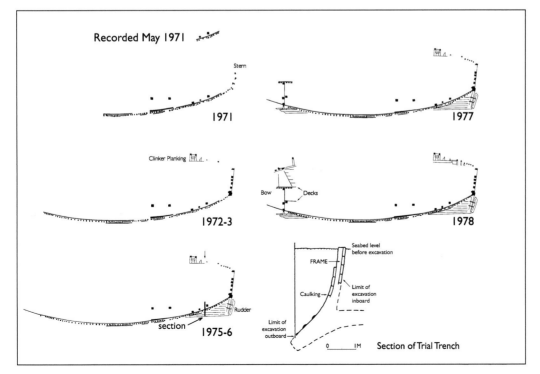

LEFT The areas uncovered and explored in successive years in the 1970s, gradually establishing the shape of the surviving hull and revealing something of the construction.

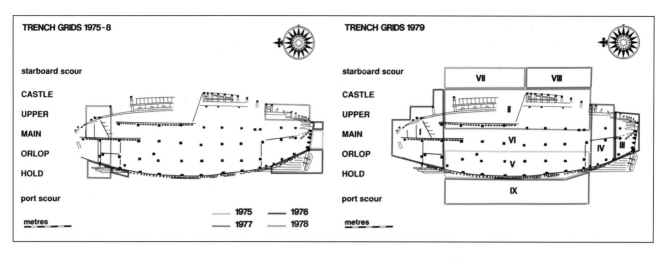

TRENCH GRIDS 1975-8

starboard scour

CASTLE

UPPER

MAIN

ORLOP

HOLD

port scour

metres

——— 1975   ——— 1976

——— 1977   ——— 1978

TRENCH GRIDS 1979

starboard scour

CASTLE

UPPER

MAIN

ORLOP

HOLD

port scour

metres

VII   VIII

II

VI

IV   III

V

IX

ABOVE The grids used in the late 1970s – a standard feature on any archaeological site, but especially important underwater.

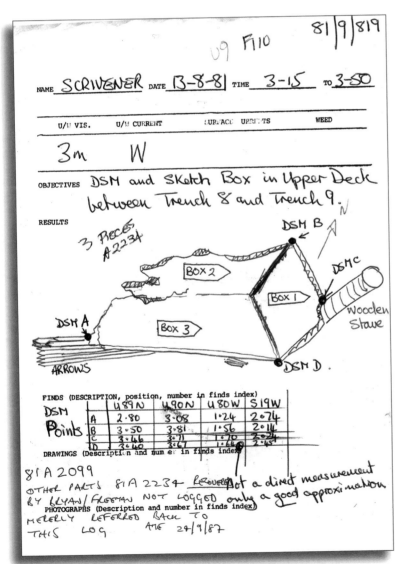

waters of Portsmouth harbour to conduct the excavation in shallow water, we would be able to take our time unhindered by the constraints of decompression and no-stop dive tables!' But in 1975 the sternpost was discovered and it became clear that the wreck was lying on its starboard side at an angle of 60°.

The financial side began to improve. Percy Ackland was taken on as the first regular employee in 1972, while grants came in from the City of Portsmouth and others, so that the budget was from £10,000 to £15,000 by the mid-1970s. The keel was discovered and excavated to establish the size of the ship, although it became clear that nothing of the bow remained. In 1978 it was possible to dig a large trench across the foremost part and to explore the inside of the hull for the first time, rather than digging around its edges. This soon yielded a rich crop of artefacts, but more importantly it showed that a substantial part of the hull was indeed intact in the silt beneath the Solent.

It finally became apparent that the dig had cut across on the line of a bulkhead running along the aft end of the fighting castle at the bow. In one small compartment, under a ladder, a long grey wooden box lay on a steeply heeled deck. The dovetailing was perfect and it

LEFT Part of the record kept of a dive in August 1981. Documents like these recorded the precise location, the features worked on and any objects recovered. As well as providing a permanent record, they helped the site supervisor and director to assess the progress of the work.

looked exactly like the sort of chest one might expect to find in one's grandmother's attic, sound but covered in cobwebs. One would never imagine that this furniture had been under the sea for more than 430 years, except that a gaming board, part of a protractor and a human bone lay on it.

A grid was constructed over the area to be excavated in accordance with standard archaeological practice, in order to guide the work on the trenches. There were natural tensions between the different members of the team. Ship historians like McKee wanted to raise the hull. They were impatient with the archaeologists who were more used to dealing with land sites that would soon be covered by buildings, and wanted to record each item in great detail.

Towards the raising

In 1978 the project moved from the 'kitchen sink' phase, according to Margaret Rule. A meeting of archaeologists, ship historians, naval architects and museum staff recommended the raising of the hull after the removal of the contents, and a meeting of salvage experts and naval architects agreed that it was practicable. The Mary Rose Trust was formed in 1979 with a high-profile group of members. These included Prince Charles, who had first dived on the site in 1975. His membership proved important, indeed *The Times* thought the support of the Prince of Wales was crucial to the project – he was highly popular, his marriage prospects were a constant theme of the press and in 1981 he married Lady Diana Spencer.

Now that the raising of the hull was a realistic prospect rather than a dream, a larger and more suitable diving vessel was needed. The salvage vessel *Sleipner* had been built for the Royal Navy in 1943 and used in the recovery of the *Vasa* in 1961. She was 43m (170ft) long and had accommodation on board with a strong crane over the bow. A

RIGHT The *Sleipner* was in use from 1979 on a four-point mooring to keep her in place, and offered far better facilities than previous vessels, beginning a new phase in the recovery operation.

MARY ROSE 1978

ABOVE A popular perspective view shows the hull lying on the seabed as it was revealed up to 1978, and giving a sense of scale of the ship by comparing it to a London bus.

BELOW Margaret Rule with Prince Charles, who became an enthusiastic supporter of the project and President of the Mary Rose Trust. He also dived on the ship many times, as seen by his diving gear.

LEFT Christopher Dobbs holding a newly recovered longbow. An archaeology graduate from Cambridge, he was an early member of the diving team and still works for the Trust as Head of Interpretation.

shore base was set up in Portsmouth with the support of the City Council. Margaret Rule was employed as archaeological director, and apart from the crew of the *Sleipner*, the team now comprised 16 people. These included Jonathan Adams who later became professor of archaeology at Southampton, and Christopher Dobbs and Alexzandra Hildred who are still with the Trust.

All this allowed the first full season of work in 1979, when 6,858 dives took place on 146 days. Three large trenches were dug by hand, while the spoil was sucked away with an airlift, unmasking most of the interior. The separate trenches were joined together that year, revealing the ship while in 'open area excavation'.

There were hundreds of amateur divers working on the project, 180 during 1979 alone. The British Sub Aqua Club training programme was adequate for normal purposes, but a specialised scheme was needed for such delicate work. A new diver had to undergo two days of training, including a talk giving an outline of the project, then one on diving safety. A video film demonstrated the archaeological techniques and then each volunteer went on a conducted tour of the site, showing the grid over the wreck and the 'shot lines' that led back to the *Sleipner* and safety. Next day the diver went down with a more experienced volunteer or member of staff to be shown how to do a task such as using the airlift to remove spoil. But there were still dangers, and in 1980 21-year-old Louise Mulford died on her fourth dive after vomiting underwater.

Deck planks had been held in place with iron nails that had rusted away, while other timbers had often moved with the impact of sinking and could not be trusted to stay in

LEFT Alex Hildred and Margaret Rule examining and spraying longbows recovered from the site, still inside their chest and undisturbed since 1545.

ABOVE Archaeologist Alexzandra Hildred at the port stern of the wreck on a day of better visibility. *(Christopher Dobbs)*

LEFT Margaret Rule inspecting a gunport from the underside after excavations had progressed below the wreck. *(Christopher Dobbs)*

BELOW LEFT Operating an airlift to remove spoil from the site.

BELOW HRH the Prince of Wales next to a spoked wheel during one of his nine dives on the site. *(Christopher Dobbs)*

place during lifting. In 1980 it was decided to remove much of the internal structure of the hull in preparation for raising it. Every item was recorded in situ, numbered and tagged, then removed as carefully as possible. They were stored in a 'timber park', a scaffolding structure with several levels where they could be kept underwater for short-term preservation. When enough had been collected a barge was sent out to take them ashore, which happened several times. Eventually they would be conserved and restored to their position in the hull. During the 1980–81 seasons, 2,958 timbers, 11,362 objects and 662 samples were taken out, registered and catalogued.

ABOVE Raising a collection of ship's timbers from the site. Twenty to forty timbers were placed in a large lorry body for each lift, then loaded on to a barge.

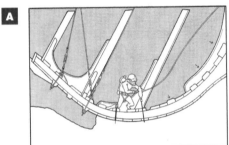

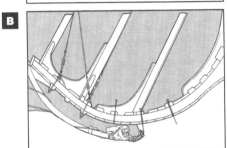

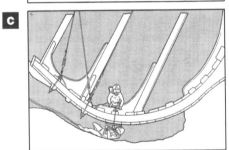

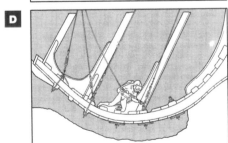

RIGHT
A Drilling long holes through the hull using a large air-powered drill.
B A diver using a water jet to tunnel under the ship and an airlift to remove the debris.
C Fixing a bolt from above and below.
D Attaching suspension wires to the bolts.

Raising the Mary Rose

Many different ideas had been put forward for lifting the hull. One suggestion was to tow the whole assembly, with the spoil and artefacts still inside, into Portsmouth Harbour and complete the work there. But the weight would have been too great, the structure could not be guaranteed to stay together, and the submerged hull would have been too deep for the shallower waters. A coffer dam had been built around five Viking ships at Skuldelev in Denmark in 1962 and the water pumped out to allow work to proceed, but the Solent was deeper and the tides were much stronger so it would have been very difficult to do this. Air bags, cork floats and even ping pong balls were all proposed and a more fanciful suggestion was to pump brine on to the seabed and let it freeze so that it would rise to the surface with the hull. The experience of the *Vasa* was not entirely relevant. It was an almost intact wreck that was much stronger, and it was funded by the Swedish government so more money was available.

In 1982 a Hull Salvage Recovery Team was set up under Colonel Wendell Lewis. A team of experienced *Mary Rose* archaeological divers was trained while members of the Royal Engineers did specific jobs. Both teams used diving equipment that could communicate with a control centre on board the *Sleipner* and, more importantly, air could be supplied from the surface while the divers were working in tunnels underneath the ship. The decision to go ahead with the lift was only made in January 1982 and there were still several caveats that might have stopped the project. The plan, as finally settled in the middle of that year, was to fix 180 suspension wires to the hull, attached to long bolts put through holes drilled by divers. It was necessary to tunnel under the hull to reach the other end of each bolt, then attach a backing plate, a liner and a nut to each. The inner end of each bolt would hold one or more steel wires, which would lead upward to a special structure, the underwater lifting frame or ULF, with legs that rested in four holes in the seabed around the wreck. Each wire would support part of the hull as the spoil was removed from beneath it, until the whole structure was ready. Then the ULF would be raised using hydraulic jacks while the giant floating crane *Tog Mor* held the weight, and the hull would be placed very carefully on a specially designed steel cradle on the seabed beside the wreck, where it would be cushioned by airbags. This was the assembly that would eventually break surface, if all went well.

The ULF was in position by mid-June and, meanwhile, the excavation of the brick structure of the galley went on. All archaeology was done on westerly tides, whether day or night, and since they changed each day it was impossible to establish a routine. Largely freed from the mud, the ship was now again exposed to hazards such as tidal flow and shipworm, which it had avoided for more than four centuries, so it could not stay there for long. The moment of initial lifting on 29 September was a difficult one, for there was still a great deal of suction with the seabed that might do some damage. The ULF was slowly raised by jacks and it was 3:25am on 1 October when Christopher Dobbs reported to the control room that the hull had fully detached and was intact.

More than a week later the crane of the *Tog Mor* was used to carefully transfer the remains of the hull, still underwater, on to the steel cradle. It weighed 92 tonnes underwater, but this would increase to 272 tonnes of ship and 72 tonnes of ULF when it was lifted out. That was planned for 10 October but postponed until the next day due to a problem with the ULF. Finally at 9:03am that day the first parts of the *Mary Rose* began to surface. Despite a heart-stopping moment just before noon, the wreck was in Portsmouth Harbour a little before

10 that evening. It was another two months before it was located in No 3 Dry Dock close to Nelson's *Victory*. A ship hall would later be built round the hull and its conservation would continue for decades.

BELOW The plan to place the hull on the cradle.

A A lifting frame is installed above the wreck and the suspension wires are fastened to it. The first stage of the lifting, carried out using jacks, freed the hull from the suction of the silt, was the most crucial.

B The hull is lifted over the support cradle ready to be lowered on to it – accurate positioning was essential for this.

C The hull is placed in the cradle and prepared to be lifted out of the water, breaking surface for the first time in 437 years.

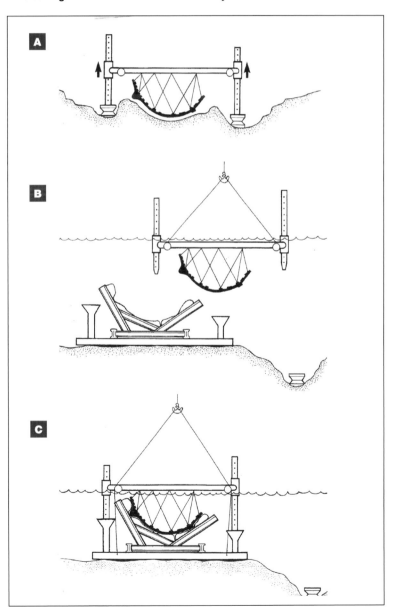

Chapter Seven

Conservation and display

The hull of the *Mary Rose* posed huge problems of conservation and display, which took several decades to resolve. The collection of more than 19,000 artefacts caused other difficulties, but many of them are extremely well preserved. Everything came together in the new museum that was opened in May 2013.

OPPOSITE Monitoring scientist Glenn McConnachie inspects the decks of the *Mary Rose* in 1994, wearing protective clothing.

As the *Mary Rose* entered Portsmouth in 1982 *The Times* was not alone in asking 'whether £4m is a fair price to pay for 700 tons [sic] of sodden timber'. Almost everyone agreed that the recovery was 'superbly efficient', as Richard Ingrams had put it, but the long-term task was to prove that it was not an 'ultimately pointless exercise'.

Once the hull was safely in Portsmouth Harbour, it was installed in No 3 Dry Dock on 8 December 1982 and work began in roofing the dock over. Portsmouth Dockyard was probably where the *Mary Rose* was built and had been the core of the country's premier naval base for nearly 500 years. It was already beginning to shift its emphasis from ship repair to maritime heritage. The navy cuts instigated by Defence Minister John Nott planned to run much of the base down and transfer work to Plymouth and Faslane in Scotland, although these intentions were partly reversed after the Falklands War. The dockyard had contained

Nelson's flagship *Victory* since 1922 and that was one of the country's leading visitor attractions. The Royal Naval Museum was also part of the complex. The *Mary Rose* was to lie very close to the *Victory*, and the huge publicity for the raising ensured that it would have high visitor figures for the next few years.

The ship hall was ready to be opened on 4 October 1983, almost a year after the recovery, and the first visitors were the Duke family from Dundee. The Mary Rose Museum opened in No 5 Boathouse near the dockyard gate in July 1984, but this created another dilemma in that it was sited some distance from the hull. The objects on display were in many ways more accessible, impressive and informative than the hull, but it was found that perhaps a third of the visitors to the ship did not see the artefacts – a problem that was to last for several decades. Meanwhile, the whole dockyard site had its problems. On 9 November 1984 the yard was closed for security reasons just as the *Mary Rose* was preparing to welcome its half-millionth visitor, and remained shut until 22 January 1985. There was little publicity for the reopening and only 69 people visited the ship hall that day, and 45 the exhibition. It was estimated £45,000 worth of revenue was lost in the early stages alone. There were two more closures during 1986, but the following year a security fence was completed, sealing off the heritage area from the working dockyard site. As a result 1987 was the first full year in which access was uninterrupted and visitor figures peaked at 360,901.

The next task with the hull was to raise it upright from the angle of about 60°, at which it had lain for more than 400 years, to an even keel. This would allow it to be displayed like the cross section of the ship in service, which would be greatly enhanced when the deck timbers were reinstalled. The hull remained on its cradle, which was jacked up as the barge was removed from under it. The assembly was lowered on to the dock floor and moved to one side. Then another series of 22 jacks restored it very slowly to the vertical position. The process was completed on 19 July 1985, 440 years after the loss and at a cost of £500,000. New galleries were installed so that visitors could see the hull. The staff had no real information on the state of

The plan for righting the ship during 1985

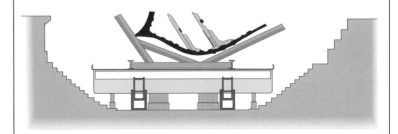

A **March to June 1985. Jacking towers were installed to support the cradle, the barge was cut away and the cradle was jacked down to rest on plinths on the dock floor.**

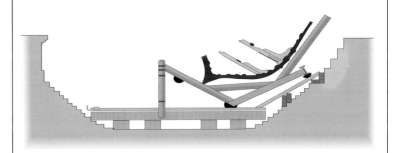

B **June to July 1985. The hull was secured to the cradle and the whole assembly lifted on to a system of jacks and shoes. The cradle was slid across the floor of the dry dock and up the side until it reached an angle of about 30°, after which vertical jacks were positioned to control the lowering of the port side.**

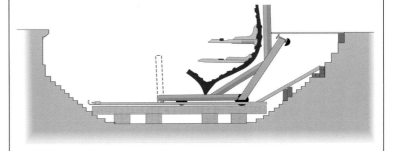

C **From July 1985. The rotation of the hull was completed by jacks resting on the dock floor and visitor viewing facilities were extended along the south side of the dry dock. Cranes were then installed to help with the replacement of timbers removed during the recovery.**
(John Lawson)

the timbers before the hull was raised and Dr Mark Jones, the head of conservation, wrote:

It wasn't just a case of copying a conservation method out of a text book, as nothing like this project had been attempted until then. It was eventually found that the outer 5 to 10 mm of each oak plank was badly decayed but the core was essentially solid if waterlogged. To maintain it, the hull was constantly sprayed with water at a temperature of three degrees centigrade. Visitors could see the ship from viewing platforms, though for most it was quite a damp experience. Although the spray tended to obscure the view of the hull, many found it to be an atmospheric experience with the ship apparently emerging from a mist.

After that it was possible to restore nearly 800 timbers, mostly smaller half beams and planking to their original places. This was directed by Andrew Fielding and Christopher Dobbs. Titanium supports were used to prop up the inboard ends of timbers that no longer crossed the hull of the ship. It was an expensive material but sponsored by IMI Titanium and it had the advantage that the difference between the new and original material was very clear. The dry dock did not literally live up to its name, and the steel caisson or floating dam that kept the water out caused concern. The dock itself was a listed monument, but in 1989 it was agreed to seal it off permanently with a dam.

Visitors

In 1983 the chairman of the Trust, Lord Caldecote, warned that finances were not secure. Recently the capital outlay had been 'substantial and considerably in excess of income to date'. Lacking regular national government support, as was enjoyed by HMS

Victory, the Royal Naval Museum and the National Maritime Museum in Greenwich among others, the *Mary Rose* had to rely on two main sources of income – visitors and fundraising. The position was made all the more difficult in that the main rival in the dockyard, HMS *Victory*, did not charge for admission at that time.

In 1987 the two historic ships in the dockyard were joined by HMS *Warrior* of 1860, the first British ironclad warship, but the relationship between the three ships was not always easy. It was never quite clear how far they complemented one another as a long-term view of British naval history, and how far they were rivals. Each ship tended to tell its own story, rather than being seen in the context of a long-term development showing an early gun-armed ship, a fully developed sailing warship, an early iron ship and the modern dockyard featuring aircraft carriers, destroyers and frigates. The *Victory* began to charge for admission in June 1986, which in a sense created a level playing field with the *Mary Rose* and later the *Warrior*, neither of which relied on government funding.

By 1988 the *Mary Rose* was still the most popular attraction in the dockyard, but only just. The ship attracted more than 370,000 visitors compared with 334,000 for *Victory*, 205,000 for the *Warrior* and 117,000 for the Royal Naval Museum. But the figure remained static for some years as the memory of 1982 began to fade, and had its first decrease in 1989. With the recession of the early 1990s the visitor numbers went down from nearly 330,000 in 1992 to 285,000 in 1993, while joint ticketing arrangements within the dockyard did not increase the income sufficiently. It was a 'critical point' in the history of the ship, as the Prince of Wales wrote in the Mary Rose Trust's annual report. Margaret Rule, for long the public face of the project, retired as Director of Research and Interpretation, but remained as a consultant. The last of the deck timbers was put in place on 16 December so the main hull structure was now complete and full conservation could begin. And a programme was launched to raise a further £3 million to preserve the ship and improve visitor facilities. There was a further decline in visitors in 1994 – a new visitor centre being fitted out was behind schedule, publicity funds were inadequate and the commemoration of the 50th anniversary of D-Day that year did not lead to increased interest in a ship that had sunk nearly 400 years before that.

Conservation

The conservation facilities were set up in the dockyard close to the ship in No 4 Dock. The conservators established an international reputation and Mary Rose Conservation Service Limited began to take on outside projects, including the Guernsey Roman ship, the Bronze Age boat found in Dover in 1992 and the medieval Newport ship uncovered in South Wales in 2002. The laboratory had a full range of facilities by 1998. The control room was used to monitor more than 100 different parameters on the hull. The wet finds area was made up of five rooms with carefully packed artefacts awaiting treatment. There were three purpose-built stainless steel tanks for the conservation of wood, the largest with a capacity of 6,000 litres. Outside there were several large containers. One held rope recovered from the site, another was used to lower the temperature of wooden objects to -27°C for freeze drying. There were three freeze dryers, including the largest one in the country. All this had to be operated under modern conditions of health and safety and protected by security and fire alarm systems.

With the decks restored by 1993, conservation could enter a new stage. For 12 years the hull had been sprayed with cold water; now it was time to move on. According to Mark Jones: 'The main problem was designing a treatment that would preserve both the damaged outer surface layer, which had been decayed by micro-organisms, as well as the sodden core which, if simply dried out would shrink and split. It was necessary to fill the voids with an inert chemical as the water dried out. The natural choice was polyethylene glycol or PEG, which came in a variety of molecular weights, from 200 to 20,000.' After extensive experiments it was decided to use a two-stage process, with PEG 200 followed by a much higher-grade solution, PEG 2,000 then PEG 4,000. This process would take many years, during which the public could only see the ship through glass, so the press and media

RIGHT AND FAR RIGHT A pewter jug found on the main deck, shown shortly after being brought up from the seabed in 1981, and after conservation. Because of its high lead content it only had to be treated by electrolysis to remove chlorides from the corrosion layers, followed by thorough washing in water. The jug was then air dried.

were invited for a last look before Margaret Rule ceremonially started the process on 30 September 1994. The temperature was raised from 3° to 19° with high humidity. The PEG 200, a treacly liquid, was sprayed to bulk out cell walls and prevent shrinkage. The area was sealed off to prevent contamination by micro-organisms. 'Although not harmful to humans, certain types of these tiny creatures will attack the ship's timbers, and thus the environment must remain sterile at all costs.

RIGHT Washing an unusually shaped piece of wood found in the bow, which could be the ship's crest.

Hence the new series of enclosed viewing galleries, which will give our visitors closer and more dramatic views of the hull, are quite different from those who many will recall from television shots on recovery day in 1982.'
In 2006 the process moved on to the next stage, in which PEG 2,000 was used to fill the permanent voids in the outer surface and seal in the lower-grade PEG in the interior. This was followed by PEG 4,000, and after 2013 it was allowed to dry out slowly.

Conservation of the 19,000 recorded artefacts was easier, in the sense that they were much smaller, but they presented a huge variety of challenges. There were many wooden items besides the hull itself, including rigging blocks, chests, longbows, tankards and bowls, casks and numerous others. They too were treated with PEG, although with some objects it would take a long time to be effective. The standard method was to place the object in a tank with a low-concentration PEG at a temperature of 60°C. The concentration was increased gradually, after which the object was dried slowly or freeze-dried; each object had different problems and needed slightly different treatment. A rigging block was initially stored in an aqueous solution of 5% borax, cascade washed to remove chloride ions, immersed in a 25% solution of PEG 4,000 for five months, then freeze-dried for a further month and surface treated with PEG 6,000. A pine chest

was also treated in borax, then desalinated, immersed in a 40% solution of PEG 4,000 for three months, and then freeze-dried for a further month.

Of the metal objects, iron was often the most difficult, especially when it was used in larger objects such as guns. Since it corroded much faster than non-ferrous metal, it was often covered in layers of concretion or calcium carbonate up to 150mm thick. This often made the object unrecognisable at first, and it had to be removed carefully, avoiding damage to the item. The best way was to radiograph the object then use hammer blows to shake the concretion, breaking it at the junction with the metal piece. Chisels had to be used very carefully, as they might do far more damage than hammers. Once brought to the surface the corrosion of an iron article would commence very quickly as it had contact with oxygen and fast action was needed. It was essential to remove chloride ions without corroding the metal. The traditional method was aqueous washing in a suitable electrolyte, or to make the object the cathode in an electrolytic cell, which would reduce the red rust to magnetite and cause the chloride ions to migrate towards an anode made of stainless or mild steel. However, it was very slow and could take up to five years. With a large number of iron guns this would mean occupying a great deal of space for long periods. In addition, there was always pressure to put objects on display for

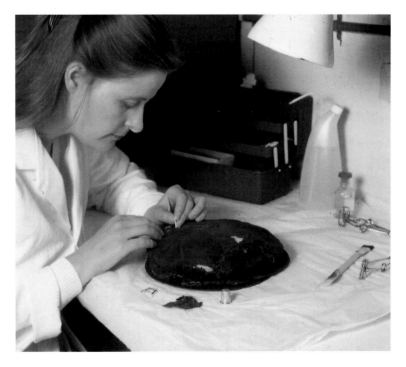

ABOVE **Gun wedges in a freeze drier, one of many types of conservation equipment used for the artefacts.**

publicity and fund-raising purposes. As early as 1975 the project used the hydrogen reduction process, in which the article was heated to 850° in hydrogen for about 100 hours. This removed the volatile chlorides and caused the iron oxide to reduce to metal. After further cleaning and impregnation with oxide varnish, the object might be ready for display within 14 days, although the process caused a fundamental and irreversible change in the material. Bronze, as found in the large muzzle-loading guns, was simpler to conserve in theory; the concretion was likely to be much thinner and different from that on iron guns and the material was less subject to decay – although electrolysis had to be used on some of the bores. Textiles, as found in sailcloth and other items, were conserved with different techniques, along with leather jerkins, pewter plates and jugs, ceramics and many other materials.

Fund-raising

One of the early supporters of the projects was the American billionaire Armand Hammer, who became president of the American group, the Society for the Archaeological Study of the Mary Rose, in 1984. Portsmouth City Council was always concerned to promote local heritage and offered many grants over the years. In the mid-1980s the Trust realised that extra funds were needed to lift the ship and create a museum and conservation facility. It began a coordinated campaign in addition to ad hoc fund-raising from industry. As a result, income from this

source declined in the short term to around £100,000 per annum. In May 1990 the Trust encouraged a proposal by the shipping firm Sea Containers to support the dockyard through the Portsmouth Naval Base Property Trust. Sea Containers would provide £26 million, of which £5.75 million would go to a new ship hall and museum for the *Mary Rose*. This involved trustees and staff in complex negotiations, largely to protect the academic integrity of the Trust from commercial pressures. After a roller-coaster ride, there was great disappointment in 1992 when the project was abandoned after Sea Containers changed their terms radically. Survival was now the priority, as reserve funds were 'almost totally depleted', and the emphasis was on conserving and maintaining the hull. A new in-house fund-raising campaign for £4 million was started. Despite paring costs to a minimum, £1.5 million had to be raised to install spray equipment for hull conservation and to open glazed pressurised galleries for visitors. An education programme is essential to any modern museum and in 1992 this started to bear fruit in visitor figures, which began to rise slightly to 330,000, partly because school visits increased by 27%.

Media presence was vital to visitor numbers and fund-raising. Four 50-minute programmes in the BBC archaeological series *Chronicle* were devoted to the ship in 1981–83; they reached a wide audience and are still considered to be the best ever produced. The BBC children's programme *Blue Peter* maintained an interest for the early days, including two features in 1988 alone, as well as other TV and radio shows. The well-known actor Robert Hardy, star of *All Creatures Great and Small* at the time, was an expert on archery and carried out ground-breaking research on the unique collection of longbows recovered from the wreck, becoming a trustee.

In 2000 Channel 4 commissioned a programme asking *What Sank the* Mary Rose? as part of its *Secrets of the Dead* series. A model of the ship was made and tested in a pool, with comments by various naval and shipbuilding experts. Fortunately it remained free of the conspiracy theories that often distort such programmes, and it concluded that 'It was an ill wind that sank the *Mary Rose*. With gun ports open, ready for battle and the ship relatively untried after an extensive refit, the combination of too many men and too heavy armaments proved too much.' The Trust, however, felt obliged to stress 'that it is the opinion of the programme makers, and not necessarily that of the Mary Rose Trust'. It would have needed 1,000 men in the tops to make it sink in the way suggested.

The age of the lottery

British fund-raising changed radically in 1994 when the National Lottery began operations. Some 28% of lottery revenue goes towards 'good causes, including projects chosen by the Heritage Lottery Fund'. A lottery application was the Trust's main priority during 1995, because as the chief executive reported: 'Without success it is difficult to see how the Mary Rose, along with many other independent heritage projects which were set up in the 1980s, could thrive.' One bid was independent and another was part of Portsmouth City Council's project for the 'Renaissance' of the harbour; but only the latter could be pursued under lottery rules. The Mary Rose was granted £330,000 to help towards the permanent conservation of the hull, while the fund encouraged another bid for a new museum to house the hull and artefacts in the same location.

There was more optimism about visitor figures by 1995. An 'all-ship' ticket to the four main attractions worked well and the Mary Rose went from a low of 260,000 in 1994 to more than 313,000 in 1995. In 1997 the museum gained designated status alongside such institutions as the Ashmolean in Oxford, Dulwich Picture Galley in London and the Whipple Museum of the History of Science in Cambridge. In 1998 the annual report of the Trust drew attention to the continuing problem of funding: 'Until we realise our vision of housing both the ship and her artefacts in a single, integrated museum, the disparity in the number of visitors seeing the ship but not the museum, will continue.' The Heritage Lottery Fund had awarded nine separate grants for the Mary Rose by 2006, totalling £5.6 million and including £137,772 for a new gallery in 2001 and £487,000 for essential conservation in 2001.

Continuing research and archaeology

The Mary Rose has always inspired a great deal of publishing on the subject, including the personal accounts by Alexander McKee and Margaret Rule, which became best-sellers at the time of the recovery.

The Trust has always aimed at more comprehensive if less popular publications to share its experience in archaeology and conservation. Volume 1, by the maritime archaeologist Peter Marsden, came out in 2003 and was entitled Sealed by Time. It offered a general introduction to a series of books, with the story of the ship – while afloat, its loss, the rediscovery and raising and a summary of the objects recovered – was followed by 34 pages of original historical documents. The second publication, edited by Peter Marsden, came in two parts, a volume of text and a set of plans of the hull. Published in 2009 it was entitled Mary Rose – Your Noblest Shippe. It described the anatomy of the vessel, including the hull design, woodworking techniques, and a deck-by-deck description. Since it was concerned mainly with what had been recovered it dealt only briefly with rig and sailing, although there was more on navigation. Volume 4 was the largest, with 732 pages. It was edited by Julie Gardiner of Wessex Archaeology and described 'life and death aboard the Mary Rose' in some detail under the title Before the Mast. There was considerable information on clothing, medicine and human remains, but it continues to be difficult to reconstruct the day to day life of the men with any authority. Volume 3, on armaments, would have been even heavier if it had not been divided into two parts. Edited by Alex Hildred, who had been with the Trust from its early days, it described the guns and other ordnance finds in great detail, with line drawings of practically every important article including the heavy and light guns. Volume 5 on conservation was published in 2003. It was entitled For Future Generations and was edited by Mark Jones, a long-term director of conservation. At 146 pages it was the shortest, yet packed with much technical information about innovative procedures. Between them the volumes give a comprehensive account of most aspects of the ship.

Conservation of artefacts

As well as preserving the hull itself, the *Mary Rose* project has also involved the conservation of a great variety of artefacts, made in many materials, which required different techniques.

WOOD

Apart from the heavy timbers of the hull and gun carriages, a large number of far more delicate pieces have been recovered and treated.

1 Parts of a fiddle found in the hold, inside a fiddle-shaped box lined with decorated cattleskin. The table (front) and back are also made of lime wood. (*all photographs copyright the Mary Rose Trust*)

2 One of eight paternosters found during the excavation. This one was on the main deck, with 49 boxwood beads. Despite laws passed in 1538 condemning their use, some of the crew still kept their rosaries on board.

3 Some 82 combs were found in the wreck, nearly all made from boxwood with a single example in alder and one in ivory. They were not entirely for personal vanity; the wide tines were for grooming but the narrow ones were intended to remove nits.

IRON

Iron does not survive well underwater, and is one of the most difficult materials to conserve as it is never completely stable after recovery.

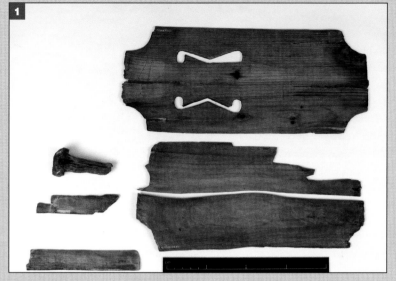

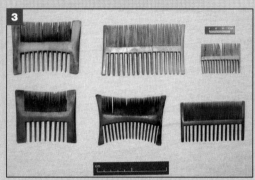

4 This piece of chain is made of leaded brass; it is believed to be decorative edging for iron mail, which has corroded.

5 This basket-hilted sword is more intact than other small iron objects, having been buried very quickly in the compacted sediments under the ship.

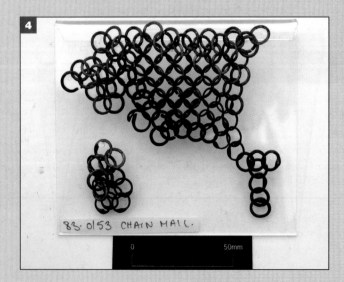

SILVER

Nearly all the silver objects recovered had suffered some form of corrosion, so they were washed and dried to stabilise them.

6 A sturdy silver-gilt signet ring, marked with a 'K'. This could be used as a seal for authenticating important documents. It was found on the finger of an archer on the main deck.

ALLOYS

Most of the alloys survive well underwater and are easier to conserve than wood or iron.

7 A demi-culverin cast by Owens in 1537 and recovered by the Mary Rose Trust in 1979.

8 A leaded brass sword hanger found on the upper deck of the *Mary Rose*. It was designed to lie flat against a leather garment that has not been preserved. The two decorative loops would have held a leather strap for the sword.

9 A bronze wheel used as a sheave in a rigging block intended for heavy-duty work, perhaps for raising and lowering the yards. It was found in a scourpit outside the *Mary Rose*.

10 A small copper-alloy tripod cauldron was found in the galley. It has been repaired at some point, with a replacement leg and a hairline fracture around the joint.

BONE

As well as human remains, the bones of a small dog were found; and bone had many uses for decoration and tools. Most of the bone found in the wreck was in remarkably good condition.

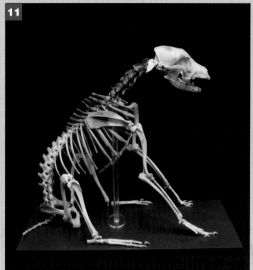

11 The dog, known today as Hatch, is related to the modern Jack Russell terrier and had brown fur. It was found next to the sliding door of the carpenter's cabin.

12 A bone carving of angels bearing candles in the style of 15th-century Italy. It was found in a chest on the main deck and was perhaps a family heirloom.

13 Other items recovered from a carpenter's chest include a personal grooming kit, which comprises this bone manicure set, a comb, a razor, a shaving brush and a mirror.

TEXTILES

These include fragments of sailcloth and 260 pieces of items of clothing such as hats, jerkins, breeches and ribbons. Plant and animal fibres need different treatment so they have to be identified first.

14 A knitted tube recovered from the orlop deck. Its dimensions suggest a leg rather than an arm so it is now believed to be part of a woollen sock or 'scogger' – it has the beginning of a turned heel at one end.

LEATHER

This category includes the skins of cattle, sheep, deer and pig. On recovery they are allowed to dry out slowly and then they are immersed in various compounds.

15 A calfskin leather book cover, incorporating pictures of heads in its design. The letters MD may represent Martin Doture, a London bookseller of the time.

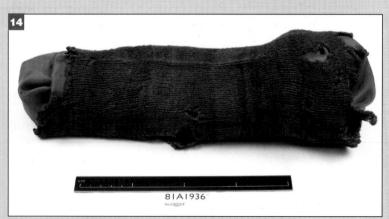

81A1936
scogger

CERAMICS

These include domestic and medical items such as bowls and jugs. Conservation consists of the removal of soluble salts, drying, the removal of concretion and reconstruction if necessary.

16 A ceramic flask or costrel found on the main deck near the carpenter's cabin. It is Iberian red micaceous ware with a clear lead glaze on the upper side. Its top is spherical and the underside is flat. It could be hung up as a drinks container.

17A and 17B A jug of south Netherlands tin-glazed ware decorated with a yellow latticed medallion inside a dark blue foliage design, found inside the surgeon's cabin.

18 A stone shot.

81A0895
book cover

STONE

Stone is naturally very robust and needs little treatment apart from washing to remove salt. Examples found include were various types and sizes of shot – over 380 of them in total. The majority were Kentish ragstone, a limestone quarried near Maidstone.

MIXED MATERIALS

Artefacts made of a combination of different materials cause special problems as materials and treatments might interact with one another.

19 One of nine pocket sundials found in the ship, of which six are in this style. Each has a collapsible brass gnomon and a sunken compass comprising a magnetised needle on a brass pin, covered with a brass-lined panel of mica or glass.

**ABOVE Information
on the 2005 dive on
display in the museum.**

Diving had continued to some extent for most years between 1983 and 1990 to look at site stabilisation, with some quite productive dives in the 1990s. In 2003–05 the Ministry of Defence provided funds for more extensive diving, which became urgent with the proposal to dredge the area to allow the Royal Navy's new aircraft carriers to enter Portsmouth. Nineteen frames from the missing port side of the ship were found and reburied, but the best-known discovery was the curved stempost, described by Margaret Rule as 'the maritime archaeology find of the decade'. It allowed some reconstruction of the forward part of the ship, although a certain amount of speculation is still needed to get a full picture. But there is still more under water and the site will be monitored and hopefully worked on in the future.

There was another discovery in a totally different place in December 2007. Written records are sparse for the early Tudor period, and it was generally assumed that everything relating to the *Mary Rose* had already been found, and in most cases published. Dr C.S. Knighton, a leading Tudor historian, was searching among the Salisbury family papers at Hatfield House when he came across a letter that had been misleadingly dated 1557. But it clearly mentioned the *Mary Rose* as an active ship, and was from the master shipwright James Baker to the king. It contained two paragraphs arguing against placing yet more

forward-firing guns in the ship, and described those that had already been placed amidships. It reinforced the growing view that forward-firing armament was a main priority and that the ship was becoming increasingly overloaded under royal pressure. Although it is not certain that the work was actually carried out, the shipwrights were clearly aware of the problem.

Geoff Hunt, perhaps the country's best-known marine artist, is a past president of the Royal Society of Marine Artists who produced illustrations for the covers of the Patrick O'Brian seafaring novels. He carries out meticulous research for his historic subjects and has honed his skills at sea painting with yachting and lecturing on cruise ships. Approached by the chief executive of the Mary Rose Trust, he later wrote:

On 26 February 2007 I innocently accepted an invitation from Rear-Admiral John Lippiett … to visit him at the Museum. At the end of an intensive two-hour tour he offered me a cup of coffee and asked me if I would paint a sizeable artist's impression of the ship, donating the painting, together with all its copyright interests, to the Trust. For some reason I said yes, not realising how many hours (hundreds, as it turned out) I was to devote to the project. But I would not have missed the opportunity for the world.

The finished work is now regarded as the definitive view on what the *Mary Rose* looked like in her last days, incorporating a second castle deck as suggested by the Hatfield document – at least until any new discoveries prove otherwise.

The new museum

By the spring of 2000 the Trust was looking at No 4 Boathouse for the permanent exhibition. The factory-like building is one of the first to be seen by visitors arriving at Portsmouth Harbour station and entering the dockyard by the Victory Gate. It was not conventionally beautiful but it had its supporters, as the only major construction in the yard during the lean years between the world wars, and bids to replace it with a modern hotel were resisted. Under the Trust's plan the artefacts would only have to move over the road to the new site, but it would involve transporting the now 300-ton hull of the *Mary Rose* 500m across the dockyard. In the end this plan came to nothing.

In December 2004 the Trust advertised in the *European Journal* for expressions of interest in designing and building a new museum, and at the same time a new bid for a lottery grant was prepared, to be submitted in December 2005. Forty replies to the advertisement were received. One proposal, by the American architect Christopher Alexander and others, was not lacking in ambition. It was inspired by a drawing by Prince Charles and was reminiscent of the chapel of King's College, Cambridge. It was claimed: 'A new Mary Rose Museum, ushering in a period of greater concern with craft, an era in which the sophisticated technology of our time, and concern for spiritual comfort, go hand in hand to show how a new architecture for the twentieth century might begin.' But instead the Trust chose a design by the British firm Wilkinson Eyre who had already won the Stirling Prize of the Royal Institute of British Architects in 2002 and 2003, for the Magna Science Centre in Rotherham and the Gateshead Millennium Bridge. The *Mary Rose* building was expected to cost £22 million and the lottery bid asked for half that sum. Unfortunately it was turned down on the grounds that the vision was not coherent enough: 'The HLF Trustees considered that the Trust needs to be absolutely clear in its aim. Is our vision correct? Are we to be a museum embracing the whole of Tudor Maritime Life, or should we be concentrating largely on the *Mary Rose*?'

However, the Mary Rose Trustees were not

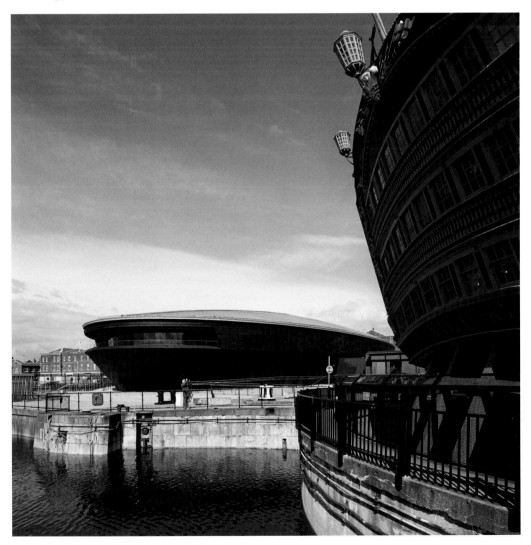

LEFT The new museum as seen across the stern of HMS *Victory*. From this viewpoint, which is likely to become a classic, its curved shape fits in well with the *Victory* and other ships in the port.
(Hufton+Crow)

downhearted. The HLF agreed that 'the Mary Rose is one of the most important pieces of our nation's heritage' and that 'such a treasure deserves a truly world-class museum to tell the story'. It was made clear that a revised bid would be looked on favourably, so Stephen Riley of the National Maritime Museum was taken on as Project Champion for the bid, succeeded by Eric Kentley as project consultant to augment the curatorial team.

Perhaps as a reaction to thirty years in which the hull was separated from the artefacts, the two elements were to be very closely integrated in the new building. The architects claimed:

At the heart of the design is the idea of specificity – both in the creation of an installation reflective of context and content, and the complex environmental conditions in which the ship and its unique legacy will be preserved. The design takes an 'inside-out' approach, cradling the hull at the centre of the museum, and creating a virtual glass hull alongside it to represent the missing section, within which the artefacts will be displayed in context on deck-level galleries. Our intention is to enclose these treasures in a building of minimal volume – a discreet and understated 'jewellery box' which will establish a respectful dialogue with the HMS Victory nearby.

The building itself would be of an 'elegant, elliptical form' in the shape of a oyster and would be 'clad in carvel timber planking to reflect the vernacular maritime architecture of England's south coast, and ornamented with inscriptions drawn from the carved ciphers used by the crew of the Mary Rose to identify their personal belongings'. It was to be 'roofed by a lustrous grey shell structure' that would be prefabricated and lifted into place over the existing ship hall.

In June 2009 the HLF announced that the bid for £21 million had been successful. The Trust had already raised £10 million and efforts were to be made to raise more to complete the total £35 million that was needed. Visitors were urged to see the hull as soon as possible before it was closed to the public, but in the meantime the museum would still display the artefacts,

while throughout the construction phase the hull would be 'interpreted imaginatively within, including a new introductory film, enhanced displays and time lapse photography'.

The new museum opened in May 2013 – not quite in time for the 2012 London Olympics as originally hoped. There is a small display on the early history of the ship and some material on the recovery, but mostly the new museum tells the story at a single point in time, the day of the loss. It is on three levels, accordant with the lower, main and upper decks. In each case the ship is set to one side, and for the moment the visitors have to see it through ports. In 2016, when drying is complete, the dividing walls will be removed so that the visitor to the upper galley will be in the same room as the ship – for the first time since the damp days before 1994. On the other side of each gallery, the visitor is treated to a display of recovered objects: the lower deck has the galley and storage casks; the main deck is dominated by the heavy guns and personal items; and the upper deck has an exhibition of rigging and navigational tools, with lighter guns and weapons such as the magnificent Tudor longbows, and contents of the well-preserved chests of officers and gentlemen. The Admiral's Gallery contains a selection of some of the best objects, including a pewter dinner service that can be hired out for functions to provide extra funding. Preservation and lighting are so effective that the visitors often need convincing that they are seeing the real thing and not replicas.

There are features on selected members of the crew such as the carpenter, master gunner, cook and archers, and the skeleton of the dog known as 'Hatch' from the position where it was recovered. At the end of the galleries are displays on aspects of the ship, such as the science gallery dealing with human and environmental remains, excavation techniques and conservation. Other exhibitions cover the men of the lower deck, the Cowdray engraving, the different lifestyle of the officers with books, good food and musical entertainment, and the stories of the divers who made it all possible.

Despite all the publicity, visitors can still be confused about the story of the *Mary Rose* before they arrive. One group turned up

expecting to see the *Mary Celeste*, which had been found abandoned in the Atlantic. Another party were told jokingly that the ship had sailed two minutes ago and apparently took it seriously. But by far the biggest myth, among the general public as well as visitors to the ship, is that she sank on her maiden voyage instead of after more than 30 years of service. The confusion with the Swedish *Vasa* and the *Titanic* is so deeply ingrained that some are still in disbelief even after the facts are presented to them.

The *Observer*'s critic did not like the curves of the building, which were not in keeping with the rest of the dockyard: 'In general, structures in Portsmouth docks follow a simple rule – if they're designed to float they use curves, if to stand they're rectangular – and the museum might have done better to follow it.' But others were far more positive and *Current Archaeology* commented:

As much an experience as a display, the new Mary Rose museum offers an unparalleled glimpse of life in Tudor England. It is easy to forget just how stunning the objects recovered from the wreck are. The range and quality of artefacts on display is simply jaw dropping. The ship herself has not looked better since the 16th century, and will become ever more impressive as conservation draws to a close. This is the closest any of us can come to boarding a Tudor warship. An experience indeed.

In November 2013 the museum won the Best UK Tourism Project award, among many others.

The *Mary Rose* never completely lost its place in the British national heart. It has largely been revived by the new museum, and it is hoped that the ship will retain its stature. It still attracts superlatives. According to David Starkey, the popular Tudor historian: 'The *Mary Rose* is the English Pompeii, preserved by water, not fire. All Tudor life is there; it is like stepping inside a Holbein painting.'

ABOVE A large-scale reproduction of the Cowdray engraving at the entrance to the new museum showing the loss of the ship and introducing the visitor to the tragedy and the *Mary Rose* story.

Appendix

Your route through the Mary Rose Museum

**'The Story Continues' signs in each gallery directs
you along the visitor route shown here**

1   RECEPTION AND ENTRANCE

2   THE KING'S SHIP
The *Mary Rose* had a successful career from her launch in
1511 until a fateful day in July 1545. She was paid for by
Henry VIII and his mark is to be found on many objects,
from rigging blocks to the large bronze guns.

3   19TH JULY 1545
The *Mary Rose* was lost during a battle with an invading
French fleet, much larger than Spanish Armada 43 years
later. There are many theories on why she sank but we will
never be certain. But we do know that 500 men lost their
lives.

4   THE MAIN DECKS
Thousands of objects have been recovered from the
seabed. Opposite the remains of the hull many of these -
the guns, their carriages and all the ship's equipment –
are arranged as they would have been on the ship minutes
before she sank.

5   MEN OF THE MAIN DECK
The cabins of the Master Carpenter and the
ship's surgeon were on the main deck. The
wreck contained a very large number of
woodworking tools, medicine containers and pieces of
medical equipment. Also found on this deck was a chest
belonging to the Master Gunner, a key figure on this
floating gun platform.
**Go down the stairs to continue your visit. Alternatively,
please use the nearby lift.**

6   SCIENCE AND THE *MARY ROSE*
The *Mary Rose* and her objects have been saved through
many scientific techniques. Research has revealed much
about the ship and her crew.

7   THE LOWER DECKS
The ship's provisions and spare equipment were stored in
the bottom levels of the ship. Here too was the ship's galley,
found under four metres of mud.

8   MEN OF THE LOWER DECKS
The ship's large collection of cooking utensils allows us
to reconstruct much of how the crew and officers were
fed. Other objects recovered from the lower decks tell
us how the men spent their time, at work and at leisure.

9   *MARY ROSE* VIEWING LIFT
This lift rises from the bottom of the ship to the upper
decks and gives spectacular views of the ship's hull.
**If you do not wish to use the lift, please go up two
flights of stairs to the Upper Decks.**

10   MEN OF THE UPPER DECKS
The ship's officers had their cabins on the upper and
castle decks. It was also here that the soldiers stood,
armed with longbows, swords, pikes or muskets to
attack the enemy.

11   HANDS ON THE *MARY ROSE*
Test your strength and skill with weapons such as the
longbow and pike.
Special demonstrations are held every week – see
notices for timings.

12   THE UPPER DECKS
The upper deck was covered with a net to stop the
enemy boarding the ship. Sadly, it also trapped a great
many of the *Mary Rose*'s crew making it impossible for
them to escape the sinking ship.

13   THE ADMIRAL'S GALLERY
Unlike the crew, the officers had fine pewterware to eat
and drink from, books to read and fashionable clothes
to wear. Even some of the musical instruments they
listened to have survived.

14   DIVERS' STORIES
The excavation and recovery of the *Mary Rose* was the
largest underwater archeological project ever unde
taken, a huge achievement involving hundreds of
people, professional and amateur.

15   MUSEUM SHOP AND CAFÉ

The plan of the new Mary Rose Museum showing the different levels, with the hull of the ship in the centre and displays of different artefacts around it.

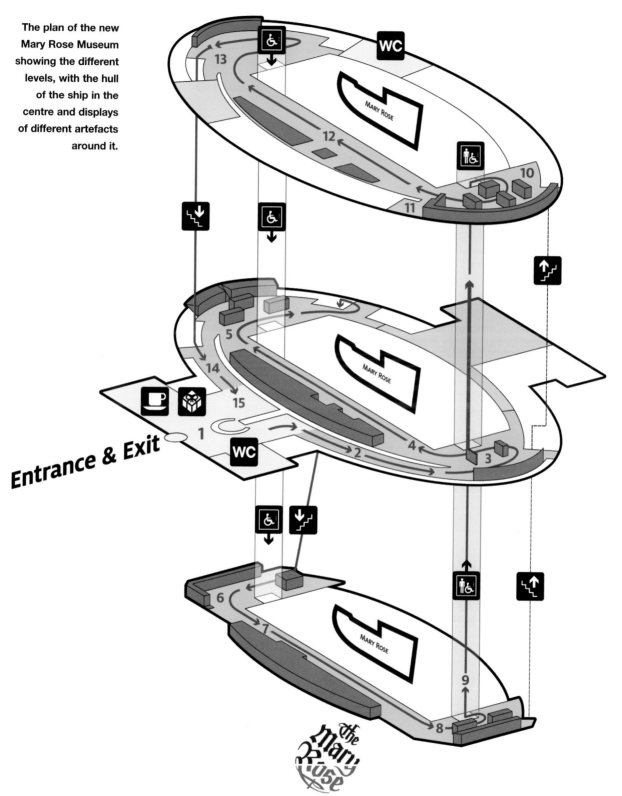

Entrance & Exit

The Mary Rose Museum, Main Road, HM Naval Base, Portsmouth, Hampshire, PO1 3PY

Registered Company No: 1447628 England and Wales   VAT Reg No: 10294564   © Mary Rose Trust (registered charity 277503)

Bibliography

National Archives Documents
E 36/5, expenses of building the *Grace Dieu* and other ships at Woolwich, 1512–14
E 36/11, , Account for making the *Katherine Plesaunce* and for transporting the King to Calais and Lygon, 1518–19
E 101/57/2, Papers relating to ordnance and shipping, 1513–15
E 101/690/7, Memoranda of Robert Brigandyn concerning accounts, equipment of ships, etc, 1485-1509
SP 1/152-56, Letters and Papers, 1539–45

British Library Maps
Coast of Cornwall and Devon, Cotton Augustus I i 35-8
Naval Assault on Brighton, 1545(?), Cotton Augustus I i 18
Plan of Dover, Cotton Augustus, I i 19
Harbour and Road of Calais, Cotton Augustus I i
Ships near Dover, Cotton Augustus I i 45

Printed Original Sources
The Anthony Roll, ed Knighton and Loades (Aldershot, 2000)
William Bourne, *The Arte of Shooting in Great Ordnance ...* (London, 1587)
Inuentions and Devices (London, 1578)
A Regiment for the Sea, ed E.G.R. Taylor (Cambridge, 1963)
The Complaynt of Scotland, ed Alan Morore, in Navy Records Society, *The Naval Miscellany,* vol II, 1912
Pierre Gracie, *The Rutters of the Sea,* ed D.W. Waters (New Haven and London, 1967)
Hall, *Chronicle Containing the History of England ...* (London, 1809)
C.S. Knighton and David Loades, *Letters from the* Mary Rose (Stroud, 2002)
J.S. Brewer, James Gairdner, J.H. Brodie, eds, *Letters and Papers, Foreign and Domestic, Henry VIII* (London, 1864–1920)

General History and Biography
S.T. Bindoff, *Tudor England* (London, 1950)
J .J. Scarisbrick, *Henry VIII* (New Haven and London, 1997)
Oxford Dictionary of National Biography
Retha M. Warnicke, *he Marrying of Anne of Cleves* (Cambridge, 2000)

Naval and Maritime History
Burney, *Universal Dictionary of the Marine* (London, 1815)
Dorothy Burwash, English Merchant Shipping, 1460–1540 (reprinted Newton Abbot, 1969)
Max Guérout, *Le Derniere Combat de la* Cordelière (2012)
David Loades, *The Tudor Navy* (Aldershot, 1992)
Guy le Moing, *Les Blanc-Sablons* (Fontaine-L'Eveque, 2012)
M. Oppenheim, *A History of the Administration of the Royal Navy* (London, 1896)
Phillip of Ravenstein Duke of Cleves, *Instructions de Toutes Manieres de Guerroyer* (Paris, 1558)
N.A.M. Rodger, *The Safeguard of the Sea* (London, 1997)
Alfred Spont, *Letters and Papers Relating to the War with France* (London, 1897)
www.admiraltylawguide.com, *The Rules of Oleron,* c.1266

Ship Building and Design
R.C. Anderson, *The* Mary Gonson, in *Mariners Mirror,* vol 46, pp199–204
Richard Barker, *Cradles of Navigation*, in *Limites do Mar e da Terra* (Cascals, 1998)
Many May Peruse Us, in *Revista da Universidade de Coimbra,* vol 34, 1989, pp539–559
Portuguese Shipbuilding; From Genoa to Goa via Geometry,
Manuel Fernandes, *Livro de Trac as de Carpintaria, 1616* (Lisbon, 1989)
Joao Baptista Lavanho, *The First Book of Naval Architecture* (Lisbon, 1996)
Fernando Oliveira, *A Arte da Guerra do Mar* (Lisbon, 1983)

Archaeology and Diving
John Bevan, *The Infernal Diver* (London, 1996)
Deane's Submarine Searches, ed Fardell and Phillips (London, 2001)
Alexander McKee, *How we Found the* Mary Rose (London, 1982)
Margaret Rule, *The* Mary Rose (London, 1982)

Mary Rose Publications
Volume 1, *Sealed by Time,* Peter Marsden (2003)
Volume 2, Mary Rose, *Your Noblest Ship*, ed Peter Marsden (Portsmouth, 2009)
Volume 3, *Weapons of Warre,* 2 vols, ed Alex Hildred (Portsmouth, 2011)
Volume 4, *Before the Mast*, ed Julie Gardiner (Portsmouth, 2005)
Volume 5, *For Future Generations*, ed Mark Jones (Portsmouth, 2003)

Annual Reports, 1979-2013

Christopher Dobbs and Martin Bridge, *Preliminary Results from Dendrochronological Studies on the* Mary Rose (Gdansk, 2000)
Alex Hildred, *The* Mary Rose *Revealed* (Portsmouth, 2013)
Dominic Fontana, *Mapping Portsmouth's Tudor Past* (Portsmouth, 2010)

Maps and Navigation
John Blake, *Sea Charts of the British Isles* (London, 1995)
Tom Cunliffe, *The Shell Channel Pilot* (St Ives, 2000)
P.D.A. Harvey, *Maps in Tudor England* (London, 1993)
Ashlin Raleigh and Sir John Summerson, *A Description of the Maps and Architectural Drawings... now at Hatfield House* (Oxford, 1971)
A.W.H. Robinson, *The Changing Navigation Routes of the Thames Estuary*, in *Journal of Navigation* (1951)
David Waters, *The Art of Navigation in England in Elizabethan and Early Stuart Times,* 3 vols (Greenwich, 1978)

Other
H.L. Blackmore, *The Armouries of the Tower of London,* vol I, *Ordnance* (London, 1976)
Irene de Groot and Robert Vorstman, *Sailing Ships, Prints by the Dutch Masters from the Sixteenth to the Nineteenth Century* (Amsterdam, 1980)
E.G. Heath, *Bow versus Gun* (Wakefield, 1973)
Geoff Hunt, *The Sea Painter's World* (London, 2011)
B. Sandahl, *Middle English Sea Terms,* 3 vols (Upsala, 1951–82)
Timothy Wilson, *Flags at Sea* (Greenwich, 1986)

Index

General

Ackland, Percy 124, 126
Adams, Jonathan 128
Admirals 59, 61, 65, 115, 117
Alexander, Christopher 147
Anchors and anchoring 70-71, 76, 87-89, 96-97, 139
  dragging 88
Anne of Brittany 11, 15
Anne of Cleves 61, 81, 84
Anthony Roll 18, 32-33, 50, 53-54, 65, 70-71, 93-94, 102, 106, 109, 112-113, 116, 138
Arcana family 67, 102
Audley, Sir Thomas 115

Bacon, Roger 109
Baker, shipwrights James and Matthew 26, 30, 146
Barber Surgeons, Company of 7, 62-64
Barton, Sir Andrew 61, 64
Battles, raids and campaigns
  Agincourt 69
  Anglo-French War 1542-46 66
  Anglo-French truce 1514 15
  Battle of Bertheaume Bay
  Battle of Bosworth 61
  Battle of the Spurs 15
  Battle of Sluys 100
  Battle of Trafalgar 104
  Blanc-Sablon 61, 117
  Brest, landings and battle 1513 11-14, 16, 97, 100, 112, 115-117
  Brighton raid 1545 20, 92
  First French War, 1510-13 10-15, 66, 114
  Flodden Field 15, 61
  Gascony invasion 1512 10-11, 68
  Second French War 1521-1526 15-19, 61, 80
  Siege of Boulogne 1544 19, 69
  war with Scotland 10, 15, 19, 61
Baude, Peter 67, 102
Bax RN, Alan 123
BBC TV 140
  Blue Peter 140
  Chronicle series 140
  Six O'clock News 7
Beachy Head 96-97
Best UK Tourism Project award 2013 149
Boarding and capturing enemy ships 100, 113-116
  bulge (scuttle) the ship under attack 116
  taking the captain prisoner 116
Bourne, William 62, 65, 67-68, 82-83, 94-95, 97, 110-111
Bray, Edward 61

Bray, Sir Reginald 61
Bristol Channel 82
British Sub Aqua Club 128
  Diving Manual 122
Bronze Age boat, Dover 137
Bull, Sir Stephen 14

Cabot, John 10
Calais 15, 82, 84, 86, 88
Caldecote, Lord 136
Carew, Sir George 21, 61, 66, 70
Carvel ship building 23-25, 36, 49
Catherine of Aragon 10, 24
Caulking and caulkers 17, 25-26, 42-44, 64
Channel 4 TV 140
  What Sank the Mary Rose? (*Secrets of the Dead* series) 140
Chaucer 83
Clinker ship building 23-24, 28-29, 43, 49, 53
Complaint of Scotland, 1549 62, 65, 101
Cousteau, Jacques 122
Cromwell, Thomas 18
Current Archaeology 149

Dartmouth 13, 86
D-Day 50th anniversary 137
Deane, Charles 116, 120-121
Deane, John 54, 120-121
Deptford 15, 18, 24, 67
de Bidoux, Pregent de 14-15
de Chaves, Alonso 115
de Clermont, René 12
de Porzmoguer, Hervé 11-12
Discipline problems 14, 21
Dobbs, Christopher 119, 128, 131, 136
Dorset, Marquis of 10-11
Dover 15, 137
Duke family, Dundee 135

Echyngham, Edward 14
Edinburgh, Duke of 124
English Channel 83-84, 89, 95, 97, 114
European Journal 147

Falconer's *Marine Dictionary,* 1769 88, 95
Falklands War 6-7, 134
Faslane 134
Fielding, Andrew 136
Fighting hand-to-hand 12, 67, 100, 113
Finsbury Fields 69-70
Fitzwilliam, Vice-Admiral Sir William 80
Flags, decorations and pennants 18, 93-94, 115, 128
  paint 93

Fleet treasurer 65
Forde, Iodesman W. 66
French fleet 11-14, 20, 114, 117, 150

Gagnan, Émile 122
Galleys 14-15, 75, 80, 100, 114, 116-117
Garcie 83
Gateshead Millennium Bridge 147
Girdler Sand 90
Going into battle 114-117
  orders 115
  smoke from guns 114-115
  tactics 114
  weather gage 114
Goodwin Sands 91, 92
Great Race in the Estuary 90-91
Groundings 15, 83-84
Guernsey Roman ship 137
Gunfounders 67-68, 102, 143
  casting guns 102-103
Gun operation 110-111
  aiming 111
  broadsides 111, 114, 117
  ladles and rammers 110-111
  priming wire 111
  sponges 110
Gunpowder 109-110, 115

Hammer, Armand 140
Hardy, Robert 140
Hatfield House 146
Heath, PM Edward 124
Hildred, Alexzandra 105, 128-129
Holinshed 115
Hopton, John 15
Howard, Sir Edward (Earl of Surrey) 10-14, 16-17, 61, 64, 66, 71-72, 75-76, 80, 89, 90, 114, 117
Howard, Thomas 14, 61, 64, 75, 89
HRH the Prince of Wales (Prince Charles) 119, 127, 137, 147
  dives on the wreck 127, 129
Hull hogging and racking 39, 45
Hunt, Geoff 146
  capsizing painting 20
  forward armament drawing 19

IMI Titanium 136
Ingrams, Richard 7, 134
Isle of Wight 6, 20, 25, 83, 114

Johnson, Frank 7
Jones, Dr Mark 136-137

Kentley, Eric 148
King Charles V of Spain 15-16, 19-21
King Ferdinand and Queen Isabella of Spain 10
King Francis I of France 15
King Henry V 10, 15

King Henry VII 10-11, 24
King Henry VIII 6-8, 13 et seq.
  alliance with Charles V against France 1543 19
  break from Roman Church 18
  death 61
  joins Holy League against France 11
  naval policies 7, 15, 17, 61
  orders two news hips 1510 24
  witnesses *Mary Rose* sinking 21
King James IV of Scotland 10, 15
King John 15
King Louis XII of France 11, 15
Knighton, Dr C.S. 146
Knyvet, Sir Thomas 12, 115

Lacy, Mary 28
Langstone Harbour 46
Latimer, Hugh 70
Legend of Robin Hood 69
Legge, Robert 67
Le Grand Routier 1502-1510 12, 96-97
Lewis, Col Wendell 130
Lippiett, Rear-Admiral John 146
Lisle, Viscount/Lord 19, 67, 114-115

Magna Science Centre, Rotherham 147
Mainwaring, Sir Henry 17
Majer, W.O.B. (Society of Nautical Research) 123
Mary, Queen of France 15
Mary Rose Committee, 1967 123
Mary Rose Conservation Service Ltd 137
Mary Rose Museum, No 5 Boathouse 101, 133, 135, 140, 146
  visitor centre 137
  visitor figures 135-137, 140-141
Mary Rose Museum, new 133, 141, 146-151
  the building 148
  viewing galleries 138
Mary Rose Trust 127-128, 136-137, 140-141, 146-147
  publications:
  Vol 1 *Sealed by Time*, Peter Marsden 141
  Vol 2 *Mary Rose – Your Noblest Shippe*, Peter Marsden 141
  Vol 3 Armaments (*Weapons of Warre*), Alexzandra Hildred 141
  Vol 4 *Before the Mast*, Julie Gardiner 141
  Vol 5 *For Future Generations*, Dr Mark Jones 141
Masts and yards 23, 54-57, 120
  aftermasts 54
  bonaventure 54
  bonaventure mizzen 54, 56

bonaventure top 70
foremast 21, 54, 56, 86
fore top 70
little tops 70-71
mainmast 21, 46, 54, 56, 85-86, 115
main mizzen top 70
main top 70
mizzen 54, 56, 115
spars
  bonaventure 57
  mizzen 57
  mizzen topsail 57
  upper (topmasts) 56
  yardarms 54-56, 67, 84-86, 89, 92, 143
  lateen 57
McConnachie, Glenn 136
McKee, Alexander 122-123, 127, 141
  lease of the wreck site 123-124
Mediterranean 20, 25, 81-82, 122
Ministry of Defence 146
Monson, Sir William 120
Morgan, Geoffrey 125
Mountbatten, Lord 124
Mulford, Louise 128

National Maritime Museum 137, 148
Navigation 12, 65, 79, 83-84, 94-97, 141
  charts 95-97
  instruments 52, 83, 93-96, 148
  landfall 97
  lead line 95-96
  sighting celestial bodies 94
Nelson, Lord Horatio 31, 117, 131, 134
Newport medieval ship 137
North Sea 83
Nott, Defence Minister John 134

O'Brian, Patrick (seafaring novels) 146
Observer 149
Owen, John and Robert 102-103, 143

Paintings, drawings and maps of the period 86, 97, 114
  Anthony Anthony 18, 71, 116
    Henri Grace à Dieu 80
  battle at Messina by Huys after Breugel 14
  Cowdray engraving 20-21, 68, 114, 123, 148-149
  Elizabethan ships, by Matthew Baker 26, 29
  German Book of Trades 1568 26
  route of Mary Rose before sinking, by Dr Dominic Fontana 19
  Hampshire map by Christopher Saxton, 1575
  Holbein portraits 61
  Laurence Nowell map of 15645 92
  Henry VIII and barber surgeons, Hans Holbein 7, 62
  Plymouth Sound c1539 81
  ships under construction, Venice Arsenal c1500 24
  tidal movements chart c1540 by Guillaume Brouscon 82

tree cutting for different purposes, by Damien Goodburn 28
voyage to the Field of the Cloth of Gold 16, 67
Pasley, Sir Charles 121
Paule, Venetian diver Peter 120
Pilots (lodesman) 66, 96-97
Plantagenet, Capt Arthur 14, 97
Plymouth 13-14, 81, 134
Plymouth Sound 76, 81, 89
  Portland 97
Portsmouth City Council 126, 128, 140-141
Portsmouth Harbour 6, 11, 18-19, 46, 67-68, 82, 126, 130-131, 134
  Dockyard 17, 24, 134, 149
    closures in 1986 135
    No 3 Dry Dock and Ship Hall 131, 134-136, 140
    No 4 Dock conservation facilities 137, 140, 146
    Victory Gate 146
  dredging 146
  Spithead 19, 25, 120
  Spitsand Bank 20-21
  station 146
Portsmouth Naval Base Property Trust 140
Protection of Wrecks Act, 1973 124
Public Record Office 123

Rigging 18, 21, 23, 55, 65, 67, 70, 110, 120
  block and tackle 57
  blocks 55, 57, 138, 143
  braces 85
  deadeyes 55-56
  halyard 57
  lanyards 55-56
  ratlines 56
  sheaves 57
  shrouds 54, 56, 67, 85-86
  spare 49
  standing 54-56
  stays 54, 56
Riley, Stephen 148
River Thames and Estuary 10, 13, 15, 18, 24, 61, 82, 89, 93, 96
Ropes 53, 84, 92, 97, 137
  bowlines 85
  crow's feet 85, 97
  hauling (sheets) 67, 70-71, 84, 86
  knots and ropework 67
  martnets 97
  robbands 84
Royal dockyards 26, 28
Royal Engineers 130
Royal Institute of British Architects 147
Royal Naval Museum, Portsmouth 135, 137
Royal Navy 49, 65, 121, 127
  Hydrographic Department 123
Royal Society of Marine Artists 146
Rule, Margaret 6, 122-123, 125, 127-128, 137, 141, 146

Sabine, Capt William 14
Sailing

close to the wind 84-86, 92
coming to anchor 97
points of sailing 89, 92
steering 85, 92-93, 111
tacking 92
warping 80, 87
weather helm 93
with the wind 89
Sailors 59, 81
Sails 53, 57, 71, 84-86
  bonaventure 71, 84, 86
  bonnet 85, 97
  controlling 84-85
  foresail 57, 84, 92
  fore topsail 57
  mainsail 57, 71, 84
  main topgallant 57
  main topsail 57
  mizzen 71, 84, 85-86
  sailcloth 84-85
  square 57, 85-86
  spritsail 57, 84-86
  the leech 86
  topgallants 84
  topsails 71, 84, 92
  triangular (lateen) 57, 84-85, 92
St Michael's Bay, France 82
Sandbars 83, 95
Sawyers 26
Scottish fleet 15
Sea Containers 140
Seamen 26, 70, 80, 82, 92, 110
  corporal punishment 65
  enemy prisoners 67
  merchant 65
  Prest money 66-67
  recruitment 14, 65-66
    impressment 66-67
  Rules of Oleron 65
  training 65
  wages 67
  watches 77
Seppings, Robert 49
Sherburn, Sir Henry 15
Sheringham, Commander 121
  chart, 1841 121, 123
Ships
  Cordelière 12-13, 112, 115
  Descharge 100
  Elizabeth 65
  Gabriel Royal 18
  Great Bark 15, 18-19
  Great Galley 15, 19
  Henri Grace à Dieu (Great Harry) 8, 18, 20, 26, 62, 65, 70-71, 80, 114, 116
  Jesus of Lubeck 19, 120
  John Baptist 18
  Kathrin Prow 91
  Lesser Bark 15
  Louise 12-13
  Margaret 10
  Mary Celeste 149
  Mary George 91
  Mary James 12
  Nicholas of Hampton 14, 97
  Peter Pomegranate 10, 13, 15, 18, 24, 26, 81, 116

Queen 12
Regent 11-13, 24, 112, 115
Royal George 120-123
Sampson 120
Sovereign 24
Titanic 149
Vasa 7, 122, 125, 127, 130, 149
Victory 31, 93, 131, 134-135, 137, 147-148
Warrior 137
Shipwrights and carpenters 25-29, 30, 33, 36, 44, 51-52, 146
  Continental 31
  drilling 27
  mathematical 30
  tools 26-27, 37, 42, 51, 64
Simon, gunner Peter 67
Smith, Myles 66
Society for the Archaeological Study of the Mary Rose 140
Soldiers 68-70
  clothing 75
  recruitment 69
Solent 6, 20, 117, 120, 122, 126, 130
Sonar 122-123
Southampton 13-14, 24
Southsea Castle 18, 20-21, 123
Speed measurement 94
  log line 94-95
Spencer, Lady Diana 127
Starkey, David 149
Stockholm Harbour 122
Suffolk, Duke of 120
Surrey, Earl of – see Howard, Sir Edward

The Downs 90-91
The Spectator 7
The Times 7, 127, 134
Tides 82-84, 130
  moon 82-83
  sun 82-83
Time marking 72, 94
Towse, John 123
Tudor dynasty and age 10, 100, 103, 122, 138, 149

Ughtred, Anthony 12

van der Delft, François 21
Venetian mariners 120
Victoria Cross 6
Victuals (supplies) 47, 66, 71-72, 75-77
  shortages 14, 16, 75-76

Waterlines 31-33, 36, 41, 49
Weather 81-82
Weeds and barnacles on hull bottoms 80
Wilkinson Eyre, architects 147
Winds 79, 80-82, 84-86, 89, 92, 97, 114, 117
Wodlas, pilot John 96
Wolsey, Cardinal 12, 14, 16, 81-82
Woodhouse, Admiral 67
Wyndham, Sir Thomas 61, 64

Mary Rose – the ship

Anatomy and equipment – see also
  Masts, Rigging and Sails
  aftercastle 55, 93
  anchor cables 87-88, 97
  anchors 70-71, 76, 87-88, 139
  bulkheads 126
    barbican head 53
  bell 72
  boats 65, 67, 97
  bow 30-33, 36, 44, 54, 116
  bowsprit 54, 56, 84, 116
  cabins 50-52
  capstans 44, 67, 70-71, 80, 87
  carlines 48
  cauldron (copper kettle) 47-48, 72, 143
  chests 53, 63-64, 77, 112, 127-128, 138, 148
  crest 138
  decks 44-53, 71
    beams 38-39, 44, 46, 49, 52, 126
    main 44, 49-53, 77, 101, 110, 150
    orlop (lower) 44, 46, 48-51, 77, 84, 101, 144, 150
    planks 128
    quarterdeck 19
    upper 42,44, 52-53, 150
  forecastle 19, 33, 53, 71, 77, 93, 116
  frames 24, 124, 146
    master 29-31, 36
    quarter 29-31, 33, 36
    stern 30
  futtocks 36-37, 39, 41, 51
  galley 46-48, 131
    stores 48-49
  gunports and bays 18, 21, 23, 41, 44, 49-50, 53, 99-101, 105, 111, 122, 129, 141
  gunwales 36
  hatches 44, 49
  hold 44, 46-48
  hull 6-7, 18, 23, 24, 30-32, 36-37, 40-43, 49, 80, 111, 120, 141
    cutaway drawing 34-35
  inventory 1514 15, 101
  keel 17, 25, 28-29, 36, 39, 46, 126
  keelson 36, 41, 46, 54
  knees 18, 28, 30, 40, 44-45, 48, 52, 77
  midships 33, 36, 49, 80
  rib 36
  ribbands 30-31, 36-37, 39
  rudder 92
  steering position 111
  stempost 54, 146
  stern 5, 30-33, 44, 50, 92, 129
  stern castle 42-43, 52-53, 112-113
  sternpost 29-30, 32-33, 40, 92, 126
  storage casks (barrels) 46-47, 72, 138, 148
  tiller 92-93
  topcastle 55
  transom 32

Armaments 7, 18, 33, 141

ammunition 112
arrows 70, 101, 112
culverin 19
grapnels 116
gun carriages and trucks 77, 99, 101, 105-107, 109-110, 142
guns 18, 20, 53, 67, 99-117, 139, 148
  base 101
  breech-loading 106-107, 109, 111
  bronze 67, 99, 103-110, 117, 143
  cannon-royal 103, 143
  cast-iron 109
  culverin 104-105, 108
  demi-cannon 103-104, 120
  demi-culverin 104-105
  falcon 16-17, 101, 105, 109-110
  falconet 105, 109
  forward-firing 19, 33, 53, 117, 146
  fowlers 108-109
  hailshot 109
  heavy (cannons) 33, 49-50, 101, 105, 117, 148
  main deck 99
  muzzle-loading 99, 101, 110-111, 117, 140
  saker 19, 105
  wrought-iron 106, 108-109, 117
handguns 110, 112
  aquebus 70, 112-113
  calivers 101
linstocks 67-68
longbows 53, 69-70, 100-101, 112, 128, 138, 148, 150
personal weapons 112-114
pikes and bills 53, 101, 113, 150
shot and balls 99, 101, 104-105, 109-111
slings 19, 108-110
swords and daggers 70, 101, 113-114, 142-143, 150

Complement (crew) and personnel 21, 64-65, 71-77, 148
  archers 53, 69-70, 100,112, 143, 148
    os acromiale condition 70, 112
  boatswain 52, 62, 66
  Boner, purser David 10, 62
  Brerely, purser John 62
  captains 59, 61
  carpenters 44, 51-52, 62, 64, 76, 148
  caulkers 64
  Clerke, Master John 61
  Commanders 10-14, 16-17, 61
  cooks and cooking 46-47, 62, 148
  Cop (or Coep), Ny 62
  coxswain 70
    duties 70-71, 76
  Fische, gunner Andrew 68
  gunners 51, 54, 62, 64-65, 67-68, 70, 100, 111, 109, 148
  Grygges, Robert 18
  Hatch, the dog 144, 148
  helmsman 62, 93, 111
  Lawden, purser John 62
  mariners 64, 66-67
  Marmaduke 18

Masters 10, 13, 61-62, 65, 93, 96
  navigators 94-96
  officers 64, 73, 77, 148, 150
  Oram, William 18
  petty officers 66
  quartermasters 71, 93, 111
  pursers 10, 62
  seamen 64-67
  senior officers 53
  servitours (servants) 64
  soldiers 16, 21, 53-54, 64-65, 68-71, 117, 150
  Sperte, Master Thomas 10, 13, 61
  surgeons 52, 62
  Symson, surgeon Robert 63

Design and construction 24-25, 36-44
  fastenings 37
    iron nails and bolts 37, 40-41, 128
    trenails 37, 40
  joining timbers 39-41
    scarfs 38-39, 41, 44
  planking 23, 28, 30, 37, 39-43, 49, 136
    internal 44, 48
    outboard 40-41
    underwater external 41
  timbers 25-26, 28-29, 36, 45, 48, 120, 130, 136, 138, 142
    floor 36, 46
  tumblehome 30, 116

Life on board 71-77
  accommodation 53
  captain's table 73
  food and drink 72

Naval career.99-117
  at Brest 1513 11-14, 16, 97, 100, 112, 115-116
  damages Louise 12-13
  fitting out 10
  Field of the Cloth of Gold voyage 15-16, 67
  final conflict 1545 117
  flagship 6, 16, 61, 96, 115
  laid-up 13, 15
  launch 8, 24
  raid at Crozon Bay 14, 117
  raid on Morlaix Bay 16-17, 117
  rebuilt 1530s 18, 49
  repaired 1527 17
  refits 20, 141
  sails for France, 1545 19
The Great Race 1513 90-91
  to Scotland 1513 15
  visited by King Charles V of Spain 16

Recovery and conservation of the wreck 119-150
  archaeology and research 122, 124-128, 131, 141
    areas uncovered and explored 125
  artefacts recovered 23, 72-77, 121, 126, 133, 135, 137-138, 140, 142-145, 148-151
    barber-surgeon's chest and instruments 63-64

bowls, cups and tableware 62, 64, 72-75, 77, 138-139, 145
    clothing 59, 139, 141, 144, 150
    personal objects 142-145, 148
    shoes 76-77
  by the Deane brothers 116, 120-121, 123, 143
    and Edwards, William 1836 143
  boats and vessels used 125
    barge TOW1 6
    catamaran Roger Grenville 125
    floating crane Tog Mor 6, 119, 131
    Sleipner 119, 127-128, 130
  conservation 133-149
    alloys 143
    bone 144
    bronze 140
    ceramics 139, 145
    iron objects 139, 142
    leather 143
    silver 143
    stone 145
    textiles 139-140, 144
    wood 142
  discovery of wreck site 120, 124
  diving on the wreck 120, 123-130, 146, 148, 150
    helmets 119-122
    SCUBA 122
  excavating the site 124, 150
  finances and fundraising 126, 135, 137, 140-141
    Heritage Lottery Fund (HLF) 141, 147-148
  guns and weapons recovered 104, 112-113, 116, 120-121, 128, 139, 148
  hull and parts recovered 6-7, 33, 40, 119-120, 125-127, 130, 133-135, 137, 140-141, 148
    deck parts and timbers 36, 48, 50, 121, 126, 130, 135-137
    polyethylene glycol (PEG) treatment 137-139
    raised upright 135-136
    sprayed with water 134, 136, 140
  lifting frame (ULF)/cradle 6, 131, 134-135
  protecting the wreck 124
  raising the hull 6, 127, 130-131
    breaking the surface 6, 131
    early attempts 120
    Hull Salvage Recovery Team 130
  skeletons found 62, 64, 70, 100, 141, 144, 148
  surveying the site 124

Sailing qualities 13, 80

Sinking 19-21, 31, 68, 94, 111, 117, 120, 148
  crew trapped by anti-boarding nets 20-21, 52-53, 150
  survivors 21, 111

Specification and performance 33
  measurements 25, 30
  tonnage measurement 18, 21, 25